ALL IN A GOOD CAUSE

ALL IN A GOOD CAUSE
A creative handbook for fund-raisers

Pamela Westland

Foreword by Chris Serle

COLUMBUS BOOKS
LONDON

The author

PAMELA WESTLAND was born and educated in London but now lives in a fourteenth-century farmhouse in Essex. For six years she edited a women's monthly magazine. She is now a full-time freelance writer who specializes in cookery and flowers. Her recent books include *A Practical Guide to Health Foods* and *Flower Arranging for Special Occasions*, also published by Columbus.

First published in Great Britain in 1986 by
Columbus Books
Devonshire House, 29 Elmfield Road, Bromley, Kent BR1 1LT

Illustrations by Nicola Gregory

British Library Cataloguing in Publication Data
Westland, Pamela
All in a good cause: a creative handbook for fund-raisers.
1. Fund raising——Great Britain——Handbooks, manuals, etc. 2. Charities——Great Britain
I. Title
361.7′0941 HV41

ISBN 0–86287–288–X
ISBN 0–86287–267–7 Pbk

Phototypeset by Falcon Graphic Art Ltd
Wallington, Surrey
Printed and bound by
The Guernsey Press, Guernsey, Channel Islands

Contents

Foreword

You can't avoid them – they're everywhere now, and I wouldn't be at all surprised if you are one of them.

Who am I talking about?

FUND-RAISERS!

They come in all shapes and sizes, ages and sexes, from every walk of life, and they all have one thing in common – boundless generosity of spirit.

They are the people who find the energy and the time to raise money for a multitude of deserving causes, from famine victims to handicapped children and guide dogs for the blind, and for political parties, too, however deserving or otherwise you may feel they are.

In this age of celebrity appeals, telethons and Live Aid, there can be very few of us who can claim never to get involved, either by giving or by doing.

Perhaps you are a giver who would also like to be a doer – to participate by helping a good cause in a practical capacity. Perhaps you are already a doer, but are running a bit short on ideas, or are wondering why your regular autumn bazaar never quite manages to hit the jackpot. Either way, you have come to the right book. *All in a Good Cause* will show you how to get involved in the most useful and profitable ways possible, and how to reap the greatest rewards from your efforts – rewards that really repay all the thought, time and energy poured into them.

Whether you see yourself as a backroom boffin, masterminding the tombola or the raffle, a creative luminary devising exotic decor from a couple of packets of crêpe paper and a ball of string, a financial genius, quietly ensuring that the books are balanced, a master of ceremonies ably keeping the show on the road, or a culinary wizard, producing mouthwatering food for the free-spending hordes, you'll find wit and wisdom in plenty throughout the book.

What you'll also find is an unending supply of ideas and enthusiasm, because what years of experience in the fund-raising field have obviously *not* done is to curb author Pamela Westland's infectious enjoyment for marshalling the team spirit, putting on the best stunt, function or event possible, and watching people part with their money as cheerfully as if it were becoming a burden to them.

There are one or two things I have learnt myself as a result of taking part in this money-extraction game. On one occasion I did a sponsored dog jog – running round a park with a friend's dog for so much money per lap. Unfortunately, the dog turned out to be far from tame, and more interested in attacking all and sundry than in raising money for the cause in question. So Lesson 1 on the dog jog trail is to take a tame dog with you.

I've also had a fair bit to do with auctions, one way or another, and I think they're a marvellous way of raising cash. Don't be deterred by the complexities of running your own – there's all the difference in the world between a charity auction and one being held by a major sale room offering Old Masters to the rich and famous. What I would say, however, is that you should be wary of collecting too many valuable items for your sale, otherwise you will find that your audience of bidders will run out of money. And a charity auction really is one occasion on which you can afford to trust people a little, too, and accept a few cheques.

It is quite amazing how generous people will be when they turn out for such events, and nothing should be done to curb their enthusiasm.

So don't wait to be asked. The world is full of deserving causes, and of people who desperately need help in the task of helping them. No willing hands have ever been known to be turned away.

Just dip a toe in the water. Read a page or two to get the feel of it.

Then jump right in at the deep end. You won't regret it.

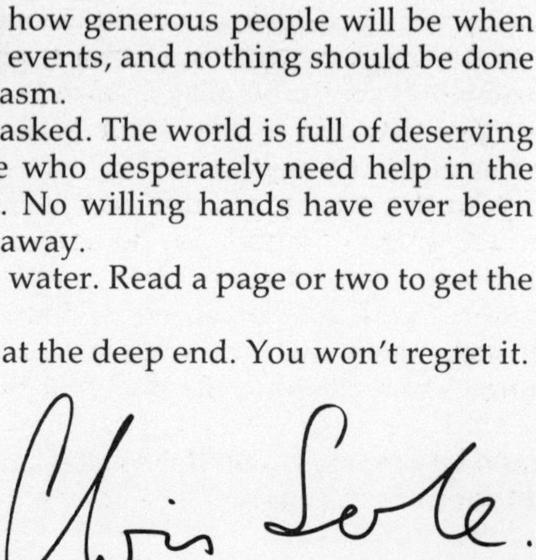

Introduction

What do a group of grown men dressed up as pink fairies, desperate to find their way home without the aid of cash, a woman rolled up in a carpet, a toddler gravely cycling round a play area on a bicycle festooned like a Christmas tree, a gaggle of schoolteachers arriving for class in St Trinian's outfits – and a lady official on a step-ladder measuring the height of a snowman – have in common?

You've got it – they are all doing what they have chosen to do, in the name of raising money.

I look on fund-raising as rather like going on a diet. If you can only find it, there is a way that will suit absolutely every individual down to the ground – and be highly successful. Plod up and down the street going from house to house with a collecting box on a rainy night and you might wonder whatever possessed you to volunteer for the job in the first place. It is like embarking on a diet of lettuce leaves and cold tea. It sounds all right in theory, and might work, but how long would you be likely to stick it?

The secret of raising money, whether you decide to go it alone or work with a team, is to do what you enjoy. There is nothing in the rules that says just because the money is for a good cause you have to make a martyr of yourself; though equally, of course, there is nothing to stop you, if that is what turns you on.

By far the most profitable way is to capitalize on what you and others around you do best, and enjoy doing. We once had a dinner party, just a group of friends sitting round the table, and someone said, 'Hey! If our crowd was ever marooned on a desert island, we'd have all the makings of a whole civilization, from day one.' There was a lawyer: he would draw up the constitution; a joiner: he would knock up a few bits of furniture and perhaps see that we had some form of roof over our heads; a keen fisherman: he would have his work cut out keeping us in protein; a professional cook: she would have the unenviable task of entertaining the lot of us to dinner every day of the week; a potter: she could dig up whatever soil there was and shape it into a few rudimentary bits of earthenware; a journalist (me): she could keep a diary of our adventures – a certain best-seller when we eventually got rescued – and write heart-rending letters to post in bottles to whomsoever it may concern on the other side of the ocean.

Every group of people is made up like this, of people with a wide variety of interests and abilities. The real skill is in finding out what they are, what you have in terms of resources, and harnessing them all to the best possible advantage. Go round the table of a fund-raising committee and ask people, in a light-hearted way, what they can do best, what they like doing, and what they have always wanted to do. They will not always come up with the obvious answers. You can have known someone for years and not realize that he or she secretly longs to jump from a parachute, learn basket-weaving or run a shop. By the end of the meeting you may well have the makings of a highly profitable and enjoyable bunch of schemes.

This, probably, best sums up the activities detailed throughout this book. Each chapter puts the microscope on one type of fund-raising scheme and examines what is involved in terms of output and input – the ratio of work over results. The schemes include sponsorship – perhaps the fastest-rising star to illuminate the fund-raising scene; fêtes and all the fun of the traditional and not-so-traditional fair; selling, whether from a plant stall at the gate or at a full-scale auction, with many, many stages in between; dances, concerts and all kinds of jolly good shows; games of chance, for everybody who loves a gamble; and the money game, the nitty-gritty of boring but bountiful covenants and cheques; all the food, glorious food and all the drink you need to feed the multitude, once you have enticed them to support your event; and hiring, decorating and setting out the gardens, fields, halls, houses and barns that can set the scene. They are all here.

And to make sure that the public is, too, you will find a

whole lot is said on the subject of publicity ('Oyez! Oyez!'). There is no sense in going to all this trouble, putting on all these events, if only your friends turn up. Posters, leaflets and letters can do so much. Television, radio and the newspapers can do so much more. They might well have started it all in the first place, alerting you to the urgent needs of a whole section of the community. Now it is their turn. Let the media know what you are doing, and why. They can help you bring in the people – and the money.

Whenever the conversation turns to fund-raising, one of the questions people most often ask is 'When does a good cause become a charity?' The answer is, when you succeed in getting it registered as such. You write to the Charity Commission, a government-sponsored body (address on page 160), enclosing a copy of the constitution of your organization or minutes of a meeting setting out its aims, purpose and ideals, and the Commission will consider the case on its merits. If your cause *does* achieve this recognition, it is good news from the point of view of tax and other financial advantages.

We are living in an age when fund-raising has never been so exciting and so much in the news. Bob Geldof, Mr Live Aid, has inspired nations stretching half-way across the world to help the nations in the other half of the world in their time of need. But he could not have achieved what he did, a contribution of a staggering £50 million, without the imagination and resources of an awful lot of ordinary and caring people. And that, in a world where hardship, suffering and poverty are the daily lot of far too many people, is the good news – simply that so many ordinary, caring individuals have the determination and imagination to do something about it.

CHAPTER 1

The sponsorship kick

When Ian Botham, cricketer extraordinary, sets off in his yellow jogging suit from John O'Groats to walk 880 miles to Land's End, it's news. People sit up and take notice. They are meant to. That's why he does it. Ian set himself the target of walking an average of thirty miles a day and raised over £700,000 for leukaemia research. Trade sponsorships, a relay team of helpers collecting all along the way and the constant attention of television and radio crews made his dream a possibility.

You do not have to be a household name to bring in the big money, but there's no denying that it helps. For the rest of us, who cannot expect the media to follow our every move, even when it is in a good cause, it is a question of coming up with the ideas and enthusiasm to command attention at least at local level, and thus achieve the desired financial results.

Sponsorship must be the greatest innovation in fund-raising for decades, and is definitely *the* money-making method of the 'eighties. Everybody is cottoning on to the sponsorship kick. People who are into getting fit, keeping fit, losing weight (even gaining it), breaking records, winning prizes, dressing up, or just doing what they always do, they have all realized that there could be money in it for their favourite good cause.

It goes without saying that it is not only the skill of the walking, running, jumping, standing still or whatever that counts. The success of the venture lies almost entirely in your powers of persuasion in prising first promises and then hard cash out of all those other people, who are not doing it. If a chap comes to the door on a winter's afternoon to talk about climbing Ben Nevis in a good cause, he is sure to provoke some guilt feelings – which is just as it should be!

Sponsorships started soberly enough, with teams of

club members undertaking not-too-ambitious walks for the promise of so much a mile; children swimming umpteen lengths of the local baths; and, a particular hobbyhorse of mine (for a booktrade charity), publishers, booksellers and authors walking briskly around central London clocking in at one publishing house after another (and, it has to be noted, only having any hope of completing the course if they had the determination right from the start to refuse the generous hospitality offered at the vast number of checkpoints).

Now everybody is at it. Age is no barrier. Vim and vigour are not prerequisites. Lack of energy is no excuse, for there is literally no end to the ways you can raise money by sponsorship. If we were to go into all of them here you would need a fork-lift truck to help you to take this book off the shelf.

Parents want to raise money for toys and other facilities for the local playgroup. So who gets in on the act? The toddlers, 2- and 3-year-olds, themselves. All they do is file unsteadily round the playground several times in front of a crowd of admiring relatives – who have all paid up handsomely for the privilege. A photograph in the local newspaper, captivatingly headed 'On the toddle for their playgroup', advises readers that for putting their best feet forward the youngsters notched up £80.

Not to be outdone, a neighbouring group staged a 'sponsored circuit cycle' around another play area. The toddlers were not in fancy dress, but their bikes and trikes were, a riot of sandwich boards, balloons, soft toys in panniers, baubles, bangles and bows, butcher's-boy baskets and go-fast contraptions. The winning bike, ridden by a 3-year-old who accomplished six wobbly circuits of the track, was dressed up as a Christmas tree.

In an event such as this, speed is not of the essence: it is the number of circuits that counts. Parents are in heavy attendance and clearly safety is in the forefront of their minds. Even so, if there are obvious little show-offs in the group, or children who cannot seem to grasp that this is not a rehearsal for banger racing, it is best to weed them out and let them circle the track by themselves. You will still get the sponsorship money – but with fewer tears to mop up at the end of it all.

Age is no barrier to sponsorship stunts. A senior citizens' group with nimble fingers and time on its hands got together to knit or crochet blanket squares for disaster victims. Here was a productive idea with a real end-product, something besides the money to show for the effort. It took the participants back to the old days when they knitted balaclava helmets for soldiers in war-time, and was something with which they could all identify.

The scheme started off in a small way in someone's front room. An appeal was held for oddments of wool and knitting yarns, so there were no expenses to be taken out of the profits. Sponsorship forms were drawn up specifying so much for each square made in the prescribed three-hour period; the rate was doubled for male knitters.

The event was a riotous success. Whether it was something the helpers put in the tea, or the feeling the elderly folk experienced of doing something useful, and in the spirit of such camaraderie, I do not know. Now, one old chap has become so keen that he is taking in knitting (for charity, of course), the group has expanded to such an extent that it has had to hire a small hall, and now it is looking for other outlets for its talents and enthusiasm. Marathon organizers, be warned!

My own efforts at taking part in a 'sew-in' met with somewhat less success. In the middle of a spate of sponsored this-and-thats for our historical society, a neighbour asked me to a charity afternoon and added as an afterthought, 'Bring some sewing'. Not having anything of a useful nature to do, I unearthed a needlepoint cushion cover kit that had been an eighteenth-birthday present to me – not, I acknowledge, that the finished article would have been much use to any disaster victims; but that wasn't the point, and anyway it was all I had.

On the day, plants, jams and bath salts were displayed on the bring-and-buy stall and as quickly snapped up. Raffle tickets were dutifully bought and sold. Tea was served. And then out came the sewing, just as a gentle interlude and something to do with our hands while we discussed the next round of fund-raising ventures. But when I picked up my cushion cover, I discovered that the needle, after so many long years in the hall cupboard, was well and truly rusted into the canvas. It took an SOS call to ascertain the whereabouts of the host's pliers, a full-scale search of the toolshed and several minutes of determined effort with a square of medium sandpaper before calm was restored and the serious business of the afternoon could begin. There is a moral to this story: before inviting people to a sew-in, first ascertain that they *can* sew, or detail them to shut up about it and do the washing-up.

You can hardly move nowadays without meeting someone who is on a sponsorship kick, even if they seem to be going about their normal business. We gave a supper party – not a charity one, this time – and friends asked if they could bring their teenage daughter.

'She won't be any trouble,' they said. 'She's doing a sponsored bookathon for school and is hoping to get through four books during the weekend, so she'll just sit in a corner and read.'

For a 'bookathon' you are on your own. There are no exams or searching questions about the books you read during the allotted period, and how thoroughly you read them is a matter of conscience. The charity gets the money either way. The bookathon is the ideal way for a bookworm to raise funds: you sit there, nose buried in a thriller, get out of all the chores because you are reading for a good cause, and then go round and collect the money. Actually, young Sarah went round the assembled company at our house, wheedling 25 or 50 pence a book out of everyone – so it turned out to be a charity supper after all.

An ecclesiastical variation of this idea has also proved to be remunerative. At the 'biblethon' held at St James's Church, in London's Piccadilly, more than 200 volunteers, including actresses Liz Frazer and Mollie Sugden, crime writer P.D. James, the music-hall star Elsie Waters and actors Alec McCowen and Paul Alexander took part in a 96-hour marathon bible-reading. If you decide to do something similar, you have a grand chance to get the sponsorship forms filled in beforehand, with money pledged by the hour (though in fairness would-be sponsors should be told that the target is a mammoth four days and four even longer nights). Money can also be collected from members of the congregation as they arrive for services, and visitors who wander in to see what in

Heaven's name is going on, or simply to admire the church's misericords. Afterwards, you should be confronted with an equally marathon task, that of counting the cash.

Some sponsored events can be pretty noisy: the non-stop disco dancing, the beat-all-records jazz-drummings, and the non-stop bagpipe-playing, for example. We happened upon one of the latter held, fortunately, in the middle of a very large playing field, but still commanding a wide and not entirely voluntary audience. One local wit wrote to the kilted musician afterwards to suggest that he would get more money and make more friends, another time, if he asked members of the ratepayers' association to sponsor him *not* to play a 24-hour lament.

By contrast, there are events which are so quiet you could hear a pin drop. Parents in our neighbourhood have jumped on to a splendid bandwagon. Everybody is giving a new kind of children's birthday party. After the Coke and cakes and a few lively games to let off steam comes the highlight of the afternoon: a sponsored silence.

Apart from the 15-minute breaks (when all the stifled giggles are released), the silence can go on for hours. An hour and three-quarters is our record to date. But what a way to give a party! Mothers are falling over themselves to book up dates while the craze lasts. And so far the kids have not caught on: they think they are just raising money to help handicapped children. So everybody is happy.

Of course, most sponsored events are considerably more energetic, with sporting achievements of one kind or another high on the list. Walking from A to B or going to any lengths in the swimming-pool does not have quite the novelty value it once did – so many people are doing it. To attract more participants and sponsors you need a little extra I-don't-know-what to capture people's imagination.

You certainly get more publicity for your venture if you invite your MP, or another well-known personality, to give out the prizes at a sponsored swim, and even more if he agrees to take part. The invitation issued to Ealing North MP Harry Greenway ominously advised him to bring along a change of clothes when he joined in the fun with 70 swimmers, from tots to grannies, at a pool in Northolt, Middlesex. And the newspaper comment that, in doing so, he became 'one of Maggie's wets' must have been worth a pound or two of the £2,500 raised in pledges towards building a special pool for handicapped youngsters.

But unless you are participating, falling in or organizing the event, a sponsored swim, length after length of it, can be a somewhat tedious affair. It can do with a bit of sparking up: a team of divers in Victorian bathing dresses, an exhibition of synchronized swimming, a demonstration of life-saving in army battle dress – whatever the local swimming club feels it can manage. Put on enough side events, advertise it as a 'gala' to bring in the customers, serve hot drinks and rolls, have a raffle, build up the party spirit and you can attract an audience raring to put their hands in their pockets.

It has to be said that wherever there is water there is potential danger. Discuss the whole event well in advance with the pool staff and have people qualified in life-saving and first-aid constantly on hand. Make safety, in other words, an even higher priority than funds.

More and more people are running farther and farther these days: witness the massive number of entries in the marathons that are now held at regular intervals throughout Britain. Large-scale events like this, which always get wide television and newspaper coverage, do a power of good for less ambitious local projects. They concentrate people's minds wonderfully on the cause in hand, and there can hardly be a town or village in the country where the idea of putting on a mini marathon has not been raised at some time or other. They can be organized at absolutely any level, with classes for males, females, juniors, handicapped athletes, veterans and teams. A marathon run can truly be all things for all people.

A sports club or a group of clubs is best placed to attract a nucleus of runners and to provide the marshals at every checking point along the way. What often happens is that the athletics, cricket, football, swimming, darts and snooker clubs will get together (lots of likely lads to get things started). Then local fund-raising groups sponsor runners to take part.

Sports shops in the town have been waiting for just such an opportunity – think of all those pairs of trainers, shorts and singlets that will be needed – and may well put on window displays, organize competitions, sell raffle tickets and donate prizes. But it is not their prerogative alone, and local businesses of all kinds usually need only the gentlest of arm-twisting to make a donation. A fast-food chain might provide cold drinks for the runners and a cup of something hot for those standing about on the side-lines, an up-and-coming manufacturer might make a hefty donation for the privilege of having his brand name stencilled on the runners' T-shirts, or sponsor a row of seats for elderly spectators.

In the money-raising stakes, people whose jobs put them in direct touch with a large number of people are definitely first past the post. A north London milkman put an unofficial penny a week on his milk bills, with the full agreement of his customers; the money went to children suffering from spina bifida. A hairdresser with clients completely at her mercy as she snipped and blow-dried during the weeks before a village fun run came in a puffing and panting last. But it was the achievement of finishing at all that mattered, and she spent the next few weeks raking in the rewards.

Of course, no one can go straight into a fun run, marathon or any other major sporting event without training for it. If you do decide to take part in one, it is best to join a local activity group of some kind, several weeks (or preferably months) beforehand. You might be able to join training runs with a sports club: the above-mentioned hairdresser started training with a women's rounders club and worked up to jogging round the lanes with the football team. On the other hand, you might have to lose some weight before you can run anywhere at all, which presents you with the perfect opportunity for a fund-raising slim-in. There have been some spectacular and well-publicized successes in this kind of venture. People sponsor the slimmer for so much a pound lost and if his or her goal is not only the vision of a newer, slimmer, lovelier figure but also to take part in a marathon *and* raise a hefty sum for a good cause, there will be every incentive to shun the chocolate and reach for the lettuce instead. (Do check with your doctor first, however, if you plan to do anything drastic in order to lose weight.)

If you do decide to raise funds in this way, think of asking your local health and fitness centre, or beauty parlour, to supervise the weekly weighing sessions. They might take a collection box for the fund, put up a handbill in the window, give a presentation party when you have finally made it – and almost certainly they will make their own donation.

If, on the other hand, you are trying to gain weight, follow the same process. You could ask a chocolate or cream-cake manufacturer to come in with a sizeable sponsorship, too.

However fit you are, however ideal your weight, it takes quite a bit of puff to run even a mini marathon, so canny fund-raisers have caught on to the idea of relay marathons. For these you have two teams; each runner sprints half a mile, then the next half-miler takes over. Each member of both teams has a fistful of sponsorship sheets, which spreads the form-filling load; not only that, it is easy to get 40 people together in two groups to display short, sharp bursts of energy, harder to find the same number willing to trek the whole distance.

This kind of event works particularly well if it is organized by a group of pub regulars, sports club members or a works committee. Two teams from two pubs in towns nine miles apart raced from one to the other, in opposite directions, and collected £700 – and a well-earned pint each – for their efforts.

Whenever your event involves use of the public highway, always contact the local police. They are the best judges of whether a road needs to be blocked off,whether you need traffic control or direction, no-parking cones or other aids to a safe and successful function. By the way, don't forget to rattle the collecting box when you call at the police station.

Letting the wheels rather than the legs take the strain has quite a bit to recommend it. One recent summer weekend saw hundreds of cyclists, organized by the Friends of Essex, meandering round the county's historic churches and chapels in an effort to raise funds towards the restoration and repair of the buildings. There were so many riders, in fact, that busy marshals at the ecclesiastical checkpoints got snowed under with participants holding out their cards to be stamped, and the doors had to stay open for eight hours to cope with the queues. Every building visited meant another 5p, 10p or whatever on the sponsorship form – and altogether thousands of pounds were raised to be distributed fairly between the parishes.

By comparison with the massive undertaking of two Hampshire sisters, the church-going cyclists' enterprise was but a Saturday-afternoon saunter. With the aim of raising £100,000 in sponsorships for the Wessex Cancer Trust, the two girls set out to cycle across the United States. They knew it was a risky venture, but their father had died of cancer and they desperately wanted to raise the money for Cancer Relief. Starting from Staten Island, New York, they crossed the Appalachian Mountains and were travelling through West Virginia when disaster struck. One of them was hit by a car, seriously injured and taken to hospital. Once she was out of danger and allowed to fly home, her sister got back on her bike and pedalled off on their planned route. This time she had a back-up vehicle, manned by friends who flew out to America on a rota system to keep her in view as she went, over the Rockies and across the Arizona desert – which only goes to prove that where there's a will, there's a way.

The higher the stakes, the greater the risks people are prepared to take to keep the funds rolling in. Two young athletes set off from London to run round the world, with only a cyclist (it was no mean achievement for him, too) in attendance, carrying the supplies. They went through Yugoslavia, Bulgaria, Turkey, through strife-torn nations, deviating only when they found there was a war ahead, and donated the proceeds for this massive enterprise to the World Wildlife Fund.

While they were pedalling their way overland, and two other stalwarts were setting off to run round the world, an intrepid water-sporter had the idea of wind-surfing his way around the British Isles for the Royal National Lifeboat Institution, and twenty-two abseilers plunged over the side of the huge Barclays Bank building in the City, a vertigo-inducing 306 feet 9 inches, for the London *Standard*'s Hospital Scanner Appeal. They took the precaution of having a team of marines on hand and one of the venturers, a nurse, trained by making practice leaps off a hospital balcony, which was no doubt terribly bad for the patients' nerves.

A 23-year-old market researcher raised £300 for the same fund by completing the Army assault course at London's Woolwich barracks – no mean feat for a slip of a girl. Smelly ponds, monkey bars and brick walls she coped with, but the 20-foot wire-mesh tunnel suspended 15 feet off the ground nearly defeated her: she found it was like trying to claw her way through a cat's cradle in the sky. She finally made it, with encouragement and advice from two instructors. Who wouldn't gladly sign a sponsor form, rather than join her?

It might seem strange to those of us who like to keep our feet firmly on the ground at all costs, but parachute jumping has become a very popular new way of raising funds. If ever the parachute regiments get short of manpower they have only to look through the editorial columns of any local paper to find some potential recruits.

Of course, there are people for whom being pushed out of an aircraft fulfils a long-held ambition. A girl I know saw an advertisement in the paper for a weekend residential parachuting course and was delighted to think that her finest hour was only a phone call away. This was a scheme organized by the mental health charity MIND. For the price (at the time of going to press) of about £40 MIND provides bed, board, training and ready-printed sponsor forms. If this appeals to you, and you decide to take a flying leap yourself, start getting the sheets filled in right away. Anyone who collects (as opposed to merely acquiring pledges for) £100 or more can deduct the cost of the course from their takings; not many do.

This raises a cautionary point. When you embark on a fund-raising venture that carries a significant amount of expenditure, do make it perfectly clear to the sponsors whether or not you intend to deduct these from your takings or will be shouldering the financial burden yourself. One para-jumper who *did* deduct her costs got into an embarrassing situation with a sponsor who objected volubly to paying for her to learn to do something she had always wanted to do.

Taking to the skies certainly makes a change from the daily routine, as 22 employees of Braintree District Council in Essex found. They took their parachute training course in Peterborough, Northamptonshire, and raised £3000 for three local handicapped people, hospitals, emergency services and national charities. As a result of their efforts, a spastic with a severe speech problem received a contribution towards a voice synthesizer for his computer, a blind woman was presented with a cassette recorder to help her to learn Braille, and a man with a chest condition was given the chance to have a battery car renovated for his use.

The para team's sponsorship takings were topped up – and their courage boosted – by the support of a German World War II parachutist who runs a business in the area. He set the ball rolling by contributing £20 to the kitty of each of the successful jumpers, and many other businesses made similar donations for no more publicity than having their names listed in the local paper. If you are prepared to risk life and limb in a good cause, write to all large and small local firms, and to the local paper, clearly stating your objectives: and you will be surprised how many cheques (many for around the £20 mark) will come in. That is easy money – easier than making that jump, anyway.

Our local pub happens to be run by an ex-paratrooper and he got a 10-man team together to train at Ipswich, in Suffolk. He assures me that charity-jumping is a good deal easier than the 'real thing', especially as it is not usually done over enemy territory. The trainers will not let you jump if the windspeed is more than 10 knots, or if there is cloud below 2000 feet, the height from which you jump. You practise rolling-over and landing techniques over and over again from 4 feet 6 inch and 6 feet walls, and once you can do that properly time and again – or so I am assured, on excellent authority – you can do anything. You will still face a moment of gripping terror when you make a real jump – but as one experienced jumper said, 'That's the fun of it. What would be the point of doing it if it was just ordinary?'

These lads raised the money by fair means or foul: mostly foul, as they used a bit of subtle psychology in starting off each sponsor sheet with a false name and a pledge of £10 per jump. With that kind of example at the head of the page, only a real tightwad could have promised less than a couple of pounds.

'It did one thing,' I'm told. 'It cut out the 50-pence pledges. We didn't get any of those.' What they did get was a total of £800 to go towards a new pavilion for the village playing-field. They might have got more. There was a 'break' clause: double your money if anyone jumped and broke a leg in the process. Luckily, no one did. Incidentally, all the participants were well insured – another point worth noting.

That same group, having built up the comradeship that perhaps only sharing such dare-devil activity can, formed the 'Bundle-of-washing club' – the name being a vivid description of an unopened parachute. Their aim was to think up the most outrageous fund-raising scheme they could, one that would ensure, by its very eccentricity, national TV coverage.

What they decided, these hefty, rugby-playing lads, was that they would dress up as pink fairies – in tights, T-shirts and net tutus, with magic wands aloft (costumes courtesy of one of the wives, who was in the rag trade), be driven in pairs, blindfolded, to be deposited 50 or so miles away from home, or rather, from the pub which served as their home-from-home. There was to be no cheating – no money folded under the watchstrap to make the return journey simpler, and no peeking out of the blindfolds as they were driven along. The pub landlord had taken the precaution of getting wide-ranging radio and local TV coverage for several days before 'Pink Sunday', so the fairies' arrival, in places as diverse as Petticoat Lane, the Isle of Dogs, Wembley market, the Isle of Sheppey and various estuary mudflats, did not come as a total surprise to the locals. In fact, people were ready and waiting for them. Mounted police in Petticoat Lane cleared a way for them and stallholders started a voluntary whip-round for the fund. A publican down by the river rushed out with the offer of free drinks and sandwiches, and at every 'liberation point' someone turned up who had heard about the stunt on the radio and was anxious to join in the fun. The fairies' goal was to get back to base as quickly as possible – and there was no shortage of lifts for the pink persons. One elderly couple, who said they had not seen such a sight since a concert party during the war, insisted on driving a couple of chaps the whole way back, and then stayed on for the reception party.

Television presenter Michael Aspel got to hear of the exploit and invited the intrepid fairies to appear on his Friday-evening show. They swear that tip-toeing across the studio under the full glare of the lights and with the cameras zooming in on their every dimple was even more terrifying than being dumped in their embarrassing garb without money in the middle of nowhere.

One pink fairy had had the temerity to try to bribe his driver with a £10 note to let him know their destination, so that he could have a car waiting. That was against the rules, and his driver welshed on him. A solicitor's clerk and a magistrate – in full wig and gown – were waiting for the culprit when he arrived home at 2.30 am. A courtroom was set up then and there in the pub, and the prisoner was found guilty and fined. This gave the fund another £10. It was ultimately to total £1000.

You would think that the wives of the tutu'd ones would have had the good sense to keep a low profile. Not a bit of it. They wanted a slice of the action. So off they went, 18 of them in a coach, dressed in black leotards and T-shirts emblazoned with a spider's-web motif. They had only bargained for a five-mile hitch back to base (women supposedly being the weaker sex), but the driver had other instructions: Southend Pier must have been a good 30 miles away.

The spiders were almost trapped in the web they had spun. It rained. Some of the girls got fed up and grizzled. Some wandered into the less touristy parts of the town by mistake – and one kindly soul gave them a lift in the other direction. Some cheated, by collecting money for their train fare home. But they got their just desserts: the train broke down and they could have walked it quicker.

They all made it back eventually, by 9.30 pm. And they had all managed to track down the 21 items they were required to find on a treasure hunt as they went – for these were black widow spiders with distinctly magpie tendencies. Stones and shells were easy enough, but a cricketer's 'box' posed a bit more of a problem. The top prize for audacity went to the girl who wheedled this article out of a high-ranking member of the police cricket team. It was returned later by post with a suitable letter of thanks and a photograph of a particularly well-protected black insect!

At the time of writing, the pledge money is still coming in, and the girls hope to top the £1000 raised by the boys.

If dressing up as a member of the animal kingdom does not appeal to you, you could always get paid for sitting quietly observing wildlife in its natural habitat. The Royal Society for the Protection of Birds runs a sponsored bird-watch scheme. Sponsors pledge so much for each different species you spot in a day. Off you go, to whichever location you think will prove most lucrative, binoculars, sandwiches and flask in hand, and mark down on your form each different bird that flits into view. Not realizing how many species frequented the Essex marshes, and vastly underestimating my friend's ability to identify them, even with the aid of the hefty fieldguide she took with her, I found myself well out of pocket when I signed a sponsorship form recently.

If your interest is more in flora than in fauna, you could organize a similar scheme for wild-flower spotting (not picking). Participants select their own spot: it can be woodland, waste ground or meadows, and it does not matter how wild the flowers are. It is incredible how many there are still to be found, despite prairie-farming techniques and harmful sprays. This idea is absolutely tailor-made for conservation or preservation groups, and is a scheme in which anyone can take part (knowledgeable children have been known to beat adults hands-down at this game).

Gardeners have been somewhat slow to maximize on the potential of all their 'best-in-show' cabbages, marrows and pumpkins, and for generations they have been content with a prize roughly equivalent to the cost of a packet of seeds, plus the occasional silver eggcup to put on the mantelpiece. Not any more! There is big sponsorship money in gardening.

What you do, as you are going to put your mammoth fruit, vegetables and flowers into the show anyway, is draw up sponsorship forms for so much per unit of growth well in advance, before you have the slightest idea how the season will treat you. (In our village, even a day or so before the show, the eventual winners will take oaths that they have nothing worth putting in. Then they walk off with 22 first prizes and the cup.) Win or lose a coveted rosette, *you* can walk off with a handsome sum for charity. While marrows or pumpkins can be sponsored by the pound (weight), runner-bean pledges are usually for so much per inch, and points gained in the collection-of-vegetables category (it seems to be every gardener's idea of Heaven to win that) can also provide the basis for a pledge. Even flowers can be sponsored – for example, so much an inch in circumference of the prize dahlia.

Little do you know that the growers have been feeding their wretched produce gargantuan doses of fertilizer for weeks beforehand. So sponsors, be warned: this is a vicious trap for the unwary. But it is all good, clean fun, and gardeners are kindly folk, so they will probably put some of their takings back into the horticultural society. Otherwise there might not be a show next year – and that would never do.

On a seasonal note, one of the most enjoyable sponsorships I ever took part in was a 'build-a-snowman' one. One member of our committee dreamed up the idea on a balmy autumn day when we could hardly remember what snow looked like. We drew up the forms, for so much per foot of snowman built, and phoned round to get willing helpers. (It is easier to do this in good weather than when the wind is actually whistling in from Siberia. Folks can turn out to be mighty busy at times like that.) We did rather well, in fact. Then we sat back and waited.

The day came, and as luck would have it, it was a Saturday. We met, wearing our thermal underwear, several sweaters, gloves and scarves, in the garden of a largish house. It was a really raw day. We formed teams, each consisting of two adults and two children. Wheelbarrows to cart the snow from ever-increasing distances were allowed, and so were step-ladders when the icy gentlemen reached giant proportions. And to keep the workers willing, it was my job to go round with the mulled wine (for the adults) and hot cocoa (for the children).

A referee was on hand to measure the efforts and sign the sponsorship forms. This was essential: people who sat at home sensibly by their fires could not quite believe that our 'man' reached 11 feet in his unstockinged feet, but there was the signature to prove it. Afterwards we were asked into the kitchen, leaving our wellingtons at the door, for more hot drinks to keep the party spirit going while we trudged from house to house collecting our spoils. The occasion raised well over £100 for our political party funds, *and* we got our photographs in the paper.

What you do to attract sponsorship depends simply on what turns you on. Some people raise funds by seeing how far their model aeroplanes can fly. Others kick a ball into a net, charging so much a goal for every penalty kick. Others fly kites as far and for as long as possible, often taking the opportunity of painting the logo or slogan of a local firm on the sides. Some people go in for marathon games of snooker or tennis. For such events you should try to get a local sports personality or sports writer to turn up, or to take part if possible. Newspapers will give you even more space if the news item involves someone well known.

Some people make a money-spinner out of doing what comes naturally. A 20-year-old radio presenter had the idea of raising money for charity in the most enjoyable way possible – by trying to beat the world record for kissing the largest number of women in the fastest possible time. He set himself up in a Bristol shopping centre, confident that at least half the university's student population would turn up to pay 10p for the privilege. They didn't. So he set off on a frantic chase round the shops, along bus queues, asking every woman in sight if she would mind kissing him. He could not afford to waste too much time being persuasive, as the record he was trying to beat stood at well over 4000. Not everyone responded with the true spirit of friendship, and some of the women he approached backed away nervously. But by the end of eight frenetic hours he had kissed 2400 women. Although he had not come anywhere near the record, he assured listeners that he had enjoyed every minute. And a group of local charities became £365 better off as a result.

A Stafford hairdresser decided to capitalize on the

goodwill in his salon by offering his clients an extra service for a week – a cuddle for the cheap-at-half-the-price sum of 10 pence. Here the response was more enthusiastic, besides being less problematic in terms of the initial approaches, and after six days £309 was on its way to the Ethiopian appeal. Going for a cut-and-blow-dry the following week must have seemed a bit dull after that.

It only goes to show that whatever you decide to do in life, somebody somewhere is willing to pay you for doing it – even kissing and cuddling – if it is all in a good cause.

Obviously there is no shortage of good ideas around. The important thing is to maximize their potential and collect as much money as possible. There is no point in going to all the trouble of forging up and down the length of the swimming-pool, knitting your heart out or jumping from a great height for a few pence. On the practical side, take care that your sponsorship forms are drawn up properly, with a column for the name and address of the sponsor, one for the amount they are prepared to pay for a successful parachute jump, a mile run, or whatever, and one for the achieved result. Head the forms with details of the fund-raising purpose and your own name. It is more appealing – literally – for a sponsor to be reminded on the point of signing that the money is going to help people less fortunate than himself. Then, if you are in the dirty-tricks brigade, start the forms off with a handsome pledge from a Mr A.N. Other, just to get the ball rolling.

Heady with enthusiasm, it is all too easy to spread the forms round like soft butter by asking all and sundry to sign them. It is much less of a headache to stick, within limits, to people you are likely to come across again, or those who come into the category of 'friends of friends'. People at the office, those who belong to the same club, frequent the pub, go to the same hairdressers, shop at the local stores or live in your road are all naturals. If you get pledges from far and wide, be ready immediately after the event to send a personal letter to each of them, giving precise details of the event, reminding them of the amount they were kind enough to pledge, and thanking them for their support. Enclose a stamped addressed envelope for the reply. You must decide whether to bear this cost yourself or deduct it from the proceeds.

What often happens when you tell people who are not within your usual sphere of acquaintance about your project and the amount you hope to raise is that they will give you a 'one-off' donation and sign your form accordingly. This saves the follow-up and is a clear case of a bird in the hand.

Wherever possible, have your achievement verified by an independent observer: someone who is handy with a tape measure and can run it round your prize pumpkin, or who counted all the marathon runners out and will be there at the finishing post to count them all in. No one will doubt your word when you go to collect the money, but it is always best, where cash is involved, to be as businesslike as possible.

Try to set aside time to collect the money as soon as possible after the event, while your own enthusiasm is still on a 'high' and while it is still fresh in the sponsors' minds. From the sponsors' point of view, it can be somewhat disconcerting to be presented with a request for a couple of pounds months later when they can hardly remember a thing about it. Mark the form with the word 'paid' against each entry. Thank each sponsor warmly and sincerely for his/her support and, while you are there, start spreading the word about your next venture. It is never too early to begin building up interest and capitalizing on goodwill.

CHAPTER 2

Temporary accommodation

'Support the Scanner Appeal – Midsummer Madness Fête and Fair. Pony rides, banger barbecue, ice-cream parlour, balloon race, fancy-dress parade, stalls and sideshows. Saturday, 14 June, 2 pm, in the walled garden, South Place (if wet, in the church hall).'

Read the poster and you can see it all. All the fun of the fête and fairground under a glorious blue sky in a lovely garden setting. And then – oh dear: the letdown of the necessary alternative arrangements in the event of a downpour (shame about the pony rides!).

If you could be a fly on the wall at a typical fund-raising committee meeting, you would find that the discussion about where to hold the event can be as heated and prolonged as the initial cut-and-thrust over what type of event to stage. Naturally, it is no good having wonderful airy-fairy ideas about an idyllic garden party if the only suitable garden is way off the beaten track, parking is impossible and there are no fallback facilities in case of rain. You just have to be practical – so practical, indeed, that it is often best to start from the standpoint of what suitable halls, houses, barns, gardens and fields are available for functions, and *then* decide how best to fill them. You are not short of ideas, surely?

On one of our committees we have a very profitable formula for an autumn supper party that makes relatively easy money year after year. There is no bother about what food to serve, who will cook it, how much food we shall need: all that is meticulously itemized in the minutes. But oh, finding yet another kind friend with a room large enough to accommodate our ever-increasing numbers! That item warrants a whole agenda to itself.

If you are not particularly familiar with the public and private halls in your area, telephone the booking secretaries (the post office usually has a list) and ask what facilities and equipment each one has, how many people the room will hold (a vital consideration if you are to be able to comply with fire regulations), the cost of hiring, whether the hall is licensed for music and dancing, and whether there are any unbreakable regular bookings. Sometimes clubs book a hall indefinitely on a certain day each week but are prepared to give way to others on occasions.

Once it seems that a hall fulfils your requirements, do not take it on trust. Go round there and look it over. Check the kitchen facilities if a meal is to be prepared or heated through there; get someone to explain the heating system to you; check that the lighting is adequate, or make a note of what supplementary equipment is needed; check the loos (do you need to bring soap and hand towels?) and the condition of any in-house chairs, tables and crockery, carefully; and have a discreet word with the caretaker. What you want to know from him, as long as you can phrase your enquiry tactfully, is what state the hall is likely to be in when you arrive to set up your function. A colleague and I were once confronted – at a hall miles from home, with 120 people due to arrive for a formal dinner – with the discovery that every chair had been systematically spread with something that was neither quite jam nor quite jelly, but was determined to remain as a permanent memento of the junior disco the previous evening.

When you book the hall, be sure to ask whether there is a reduced rate for 'setting up' time before a function – there often is – and by what time the hall must be cleared afterwards. Also, however efficient the booking secretary seems, it is always best to confirm all the details in a letter when you send the deposit.

Booking school and college halls is a bit more complicated. You have to get a form from the local education authority, fill in a plethora of detail, return it, and wait patiently for permission to be granted. So allow plenty of time. Here again, there are traps for the unwary, and I am at a loss to know how to overcome them. I once drove up to the gates of a very large school raring to set up for an evening function, carrying my 'permission' form safely in my handbag. The gates were closed. There was no visible back entrance. No lights were on, and there was no sign of the caretaker. It took quite a time to track down where he lived, drag him away from the television, convince him this was not an April Fool trick (though for sure it had begun to feel like one) and bundle him into the car. And then he forgot his keys.

We had to ask the guests to talk amongst themselves while we heated up the meal in a room at the back of a freezing cold hall. Sure enough, no booking had been entered in the caretaker's diary and no heating switched on a couple of hours in advance, as agreed. Grrrh!

If your event involves playing live or recorded music public halls usually will not give you any licensing problems. Most halls apply for an annual licence, possession of which is proclaimed in a caption over the door, and pay a blanket royalty fee. To hold an event in unlicensed premises, and to raise funds for an unregistered charity, you will certainly need to apply. More details are on page 85, and the relevant addresses appear on page 160.

At some point, check the decorative order of the hall in case, not to put too fine a point on it, a little judicious camouflage is advisable. Streamers, bunting, cut-outs and posters can hide a multitude of stains. If anyone is arranging flower displays, they will need to measure nooks and crannies, alcoves and windowsills to get an accurate record of heights and proportions. A cascade of flowers just inside the door and a couple of large bowls on the stage can do more to say 'welcome' than a banner that spells out the word.

Lighting a room – or a field for that matter – for a function is an art in itself. Luckily most fund-raising groups seem to have someone in their midst who has the know-how and access to any equipment needed to create special effects. If a hall has stark, overall lighting, you might be able to get away with nothing more technical than several thicknesses of pink or red crêpe or tissue paper shaped round the shades (though on no account close to the bulbs) or dispense altogether with the overhead lighting (usually the culprit) and use wall lights and a few plug-in table-lamps or spotlights instead.

For a supper party, nightlights or candles standing in saucers and protected by jam-jars create an intimate and romantic atmosphere. But never use candles when children are likely to be running around; do not place candles too close to a dance floor either, or, for example, at the front of a buffet-table. A friend of mine, reaching over a candle for a spoonful of salad, once damaged a wide chiffon sleeve irreparably.

Ticket sales always go much faster if a function is held in a private house. A house can be more friendly, more stylish, more attractive in almost every way . . . and often more elusive.

If you have one in mind, approach the owners personally or by letter, giving them all the relevant details – type of function, numbers, ticket price, type of food, etc. If they respond the least bit encouragingly, make it clear that you have thought of everything – covers to protect carpets and tables, people to do the washing up and clean the kitchen and someone to put back the furniture. Ask the hosts' attitude towards smoking and, if they permit it, be sure to have adequate ashtrays in each room.

Cast an eye over china, glass, ornaments and lamps that are on display and, if you think it wise, suggest that some of the more vulnerable items are put away. Err on the side of caution, if necessary. You as organizer will know how easy it is for someone carrying a tray to stumble: better safe than sorry.

Barns and outhouses, like tents and marquees, are a kind of half-way house between halls and the great outdoors. Country and western dances, Hallowe'en parties, harvest suppers, autumn fairs and steel-band dances all go with a swing in buildings smelling mustily of centuries of grain sacks and with old farm implements lurking dustily in the corners.

Gone forever are the days when you could line up bales of straw for seating, or hold a party in part of a barn used to store hay or straw. Fire regulations are extremely strict on premises used for public functions. As a generalization, all buildings, barns and all others must be cleared of any dry, inflammable materials and there must be no fuel store or other such risk element close by. There must be an adequate number of fire extinguishers and at least two adequate, easily accessible and clearly marked exits (in case one becomes blocked by fire). Some form of suitable emergency lighting should be available, too, in case the power supply is cut.

The district or borough council is responsible for safety standards and enforcement of regulations at public functions, and usually the fire authority is consulted. If the event you are staging is open to the general public, contact your local authority in the first instance to obtain an occasional licence. Put your request in writing, giving the name and location of the venue, the type of function and the numbers you expect to attract. Fire regulations relating to the 'density factor', the number of people permitted in relation to the square footage of the premises and the number and size of exits, are very strict. The local authority will then, in due course, either grant or withhold permission.

Do not leave any aspect of the fire regulations to chance, or until the last minute. Apart from the obvious danger of a serious incident, if your premises do not meet required standards you could face the embarrassment of the function having to be cancelled.

It does happen. It happened in a big way to a Durbur Ball planned in aid of the Bhopal gas disaster victims in the summer at a high-society venue in Eton, close to Windsor. With tickets at '74 guineas' (that is £77.70) a pair and prestigious names such as Prince Udai of Nabha, the Maharajah of Jaipur, Viscount Althorp, Viscount Dupplin and the Marchioness of Bristol among the organizers, there must have been some red faces in high places when the local fire prevention officer called the whole thing off.

In this case the tent material did not comply with the minimum British safety standard and the committee could not find a suitable replacement in time, so would-be revellers had to have their money returned. It just goes to show that you should never take a gamble that the moon and stars will shine warmly and benevolently – even in the summer, and even for a good cause.

With tickets at 74 guineas, the cost of hiring marquees was probably a drop in the ocean for the Bhopal function, but normally it represents a high proportion of the outgoings. Hired tents do not come cheaply, so enquire whether any of the organizations near to you have one of their own that they would lend. Ask local scouts' and guides' groups, the commanding officer of any military school or establishment, large manufacturers or suppliers who might keep one available for exhibitions or entertaining – when there is money to be saved, it is always worth a try.

Think laterally. Are there any other functions likely to be held locally at around the same time, even a local family garden party or wedding? If you can dovetail the dates to hold the two events one or two days apart, and thus share the cost of the marquee, everybody (except the hire firm, unfortunately) will benefit. It is not so much having the tent there for an extra day or two but the cost of putting it up and taking it down that hurts the treasurer. It may sound crazy, but I have known a charity function run like clockwork on a Saturday in a marquee that had set the stage for a blushing bride 48 hours earlier.

Marquees can be all things to all functions, and when you hire one you get what you pay for. This could include a plain or striped lining to match your overall theme or club colours, a stage, dance floor, awning, covered walkway and a 'kitchen' annexe: a complete put-up and take-down reception room, in other words. Leave it to the experts to decide whether there is space for a marquee on a lawn or tucked between a house and a garage. Existing flower-beds and trees – even a strawberry bed – can all be made to seem part of the furniture.

Classified telephone directories are a fund of information about what in terms of accommodation is on offer, but again it is a question of asking around first, among local halls and neighbouring organizations, and hiring later – only if you cannot find somewhere to borrow. Tent-hire firms and similar specialists offer folding chairs, tables, trestle tables, heating, lighting and sound amplification appliances to suit all kinds of functions. Crockery, cutlery, glassware (though this usually comes free with a drinks order), tablecloths and hot cupboards – all it takes to put on a portable feast – can also be hired.

When there is a party in the offing, you might feel like putting the flags out. No problem: carnival novelty firms sell bunting almost by the mile – in 36-metre (39-foot) lengths – for a nominal sum. Pennants, flame-retardant fringing, shimmering curtains, special spooky Hallowe'en effects, barbecue candles, even festival processional torches: you name it, and someone will be able to hire it out to you. If you are stuck for outdoor attractions, roll-a-ball and coconut-shy games, you can hire them, too (see page 160).

'Why don't you British ever talk about anything but the weather?' a tourist is said to have asked. 'Because we have such a lot of it', goes the standard reply. We do, and a lot of it is contra-indicated for outdoor events. When you are planning any kind of outdoor fund-raising function – a fête, fair or sports day – look into the matter of insurance, and as well as ensuring that you are covered in the event of injury and other risks, go one further and take out a pluvius policy. Then if it rains and, Heaven forbid, the whole event is a wash-out, at least the treasurer will be happy.

CHAPTER 3

Their fête in your hands

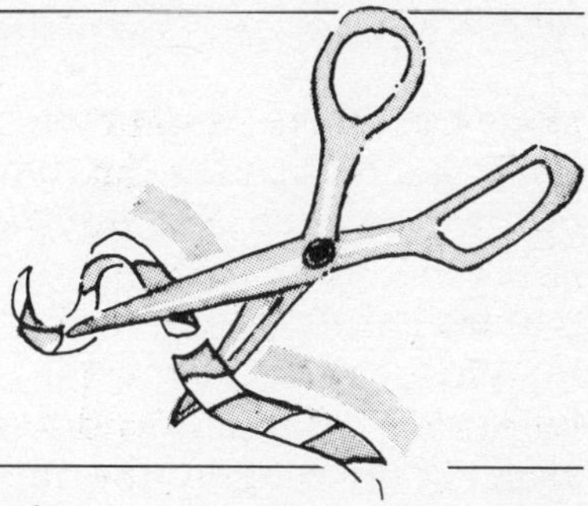

'And now, ladies and gentlemen, it gives me great pleasure to declare this fête well and truly open.' Up and down the country on Saturdays throughout the spring and summer, and then again as Christmas approaches, these words will be uttered by the vicar, chairman's wife, local Member of Parliament, council representative, beauty queen, visiting celebrity, or whoever has been invited to perform this happy task.

There is nothing new about holding a fête or bazaar. People are doing it all the time. That is one of the problems. If the fête is in your hands, it is your job to make sure that the function attracts as much advance publicity as possible, brings in as many people as possible, and makes as much money as possible. Pity about the one down the road, that wasn't advertised, didn't have any special attractions, and continued with the same old theme it has been running for years. It will have to take a leaf out of your book, and do better next year.

The success of any function depends on two major factors, publicity and organization. Publicity is more than ever important in the case of a fête or bazaar, when you are hoping to attract not only ardent devotees to your cause, but the public at large. We are in a highly competitive arena here. Although we are always being told that everyone nowadays has more leisure time than they know what to do with, back at the ranch it does not always work out like that. If your fête happens to fall on the first fine Saturday for weeks, you will not only be in competition with the three other events within a ten-mile radius. You will be competing with the fence that needs painting, the plants that need planting, the patio that needs paving and the bedroom that needs papering: tough opposition.

What you need, to crash through this barrier, are publicity darts that find their target and stick; and attractions that make news items in the papers and single-line headings on posters: the kind that make people stop, get out their diaries and make a note there and then of the date and venue of your event. Items that will make children drag their parents along are always worth a mention, for children can often be the best publicity targets you have. (Guilty feelings about not taking the kids out for weeks line many a fund-raising coffer.) Look at the 'Oyez! Oyez!' chapter, on advertising and publicity, and you will get the general drift from that.

When it comes specifically to fêtes, fairs, bazaars, whatever you like to call them, remember that it is precisely 'what you like to call them' that makes such a difference. I am all for giving events of all kinds a 'handle', a personality, a character all their own. Call them something memorable, something that nags away at the subconscious like a jingle in a television commercial. Do not just hold 'a fête', but a special kind of fête, one which suggests a special kind of feature and a unified theme for the side-shows. It is only a way of marketing. You still have stalls selling cakes, produce, toys and bric-a-brac. The difference is that the message gets home.

You need to start thinking about next year's theme the minute this year's fête is over, so that the busy bees who will spend the best part of the twelve months making things can target their merchandise to the overall brand image. Exactly which theme you dream up will be governed to some extent by where you live and the kind of subject suggested by the established societies, organizations or activities in the neighbourhood. Ask in your local library for a list of them: the range will probably surprise you. It will give you an idea of the kind of attractions you could feature. Dance schools, dramatic societies, model aeroplane clubs, railway enthusiasts: any of these could have something to offer the lateral-thinking function-organizer.

Let us look up a random selection of dates in the diary and take a look round four fêtes held in spring, summer, autumn and winter to see what is on offer.

Unless you had been hibernating you could not have missed the fact that something was going on in May. For two weekends beforehand, everyone in the area had been craning their necks skywards to read the message carried on a hot air balloon drifting over the town, and the streamer trailing along behind a twin-seater plane: 'Second Childhood Fête'. Posters on trees along all the roads into and out of town filled in the details and made compelling reading: model railway, micro-lite flying display, BMX demonstration, pram race, sack race, trampoline, wobbly castle, under-fives' fancy-dress competition (real under-fives not eligible to enter – only adults dressed as such), and to cap it all, since this was a big affair, helicopter rides. The organizers had thrown down the gauntlet to anyone thinking of doing a few odd jobs around the house that Saturday instead of jostling with the crowds.

People running the sales stalls had entered into the spirit of the theme and kept up the momentum. One stall was a tuck shop selling home-made sweets, lollipops and toffee apples; bags of jelly babies, pear drops and licorice allsorts – even some old-fashioned paper tubes of sherbet with a licorice 'straw', to remind the mums and dads of their own childhood, and how many sweets you couldn't get for a farthing.

There were stalls galore, of course, selling soft toys, glove puppets, dolls' clothes, beautiful wooden trains and boats hand-made by a chap on the committee, and plenty of knick-knacks to make the most of grown-up children's pocket money. It was nostalgia time, again, at a table piled high with old comics, railway magazines, cigarette cards (remember them?) and books about lovable and not-so-lovable schooldays characters. Given plenty of notice, people had turned out their attics and spare rooms and come up with a treasure trove of goodies, toys that made up in character for what they might lack in a lick of paint. It all made a marvellous swap shop, and you should have seen the dads sorting through the model aeroplane kits and railway parts.

All this harking back to days of yore gives a person an appetite. One of the cleverest features of the 'childhood revisited' fête was the eats and drinks. The mixture was as usual, but marketed in accordance with the special theme: not just ice creams, but ice-cream cones served from an old 'stop-me-and-buy-one'-type barrow, mounted behind a tricycle; glorious mixtures, scoops of strawberry, vanilla and chocolate topped by a swirl of cream and sprinkling of nuts, selling for an enormous price in see-through paper beakers and doing a roaring trade as knickerbocker glories; and ice-cream sodas containing scoops of ice cream that you keep pushing down with a straw until they melt. There were candy floss, sticks of rock – you can get them printed with the name of your cause as long as you place a large enough order – and barley-sugar twists, currant buns, Chelsea buns that you go on unrolling until you get to the middle, sticky iced buns, milk shakes and fizzy drinks. Those were the days!

Throughout the proceedings a local brass band played golden oldies such as 'The Teddy Bears' Picnic', and children from the dancing school staged an Alice in Wonderland routine – appropriately enough, for wonderland it certainly was.

When summer is a-coming in, so is the busiest season for fêtes and fairs. Whether you live in town or in a rural area, a country fair is hard to beat. The rectory garden, school playing-field or hospital grounds could easily accommodate all it takes to bring people in from far and wide to a Buttercups and Daisies Fair, and send them away with roses in their cheeks.

What does it take to succeed with such a venture? Depending on available resources it could take milkmaids for two Wednesdays and Saturdays in the market, handing out notices announcing the forthcoming attraction; stickers on cars, carrying the glad tidings everywhere they went; a grand opening performed by a character from a popular radio serial, complete with straw in her hair; Morris men leaping colourfully about to the music of the pipe, jangling tambourines and bashing a bladder of lard, (and taking round the hat in aid of your funds, not their beer money); a display of medieval jousting from a suitably genned-up local historical group; and a traction engine getting up steam on a suitable piece of hard-standing in the corner of the grounds.

We had a traction-engine rally once, all along the village high street, and the old boys driving them – some of them not that old, in fact – competed with each other on all levels, not least to see who could tell the tallest story. I like the one from an East Coast driver who swore that 'We never had nothing to eat, barring herrings, and if we was lucky a bit of bread, one year to the next, and these we allus grilled over the top of the fire on the old engine'. I suppose there were some people who took it as gospel . . .

Reflecting the great revival of interest in handicrafts, there could be a craftsman's corner, with demonstrations of spinning, weaving, pottery, rush- and cane-work, basket-making and trug-making. Such events make good punchlines on the handbills and posters. Some of the craftwork can be for sale – skeins of home-dyed wools, scarves, ties, place-mats, garden baskets and the like – and the demonstrators will surely give you a percentage of the profit for the funds.

No country fair would be complete without some of the knockabout fun that people always associate with the rural life – though I have to tell you that I have never come across it face to face. People where I come from do not spend a lot of time sitting astride padded poles fixed a couple of feet above the ground and throwing pillows at each other – unless, that is, they have just paid 40 pence a time and it is for the good of the cause. I do not think they spend much time, either, secretly practising at dead of night to get to grips with the problem of climbing a greasy pole – not judging by the mess they make of it in front of the delighted audience.

What they obviously do practise, however, is throwing the welly, that other popular Saturday-afternoon pastime. There is a rumour that has gained a lot of ground lately, that this innocent sport dates from the middle ages . . . Be that as it may, it has been around long enough for some exponents to get quite good at it. They take it about as seriously as throwing the discus. Someone stands by with a measuring tape and solemnly writes down the distance on a list. At the end of the day the winning athlete swaggers up proudly to collect his prize: a firkin of cider, it was, last time. There were no prizes for the chap who devised a variation, throwing a welly filled with water: but at least he took most of the splash himself, right on the chin.

Country fair side-shows are handed down through generations of organizers, and so is a deep-rooted affection for them. If you cannot come by so valuable an inheritance, or if items such as quoit rings go missing, you can buy or hire from a novelties firm in London (page 160). Bowling for a pig, or part of one (a small ham is a jolly good reward for aiming five wooden bowls accurately), a coconut shy, skittles, quoits, hoop-la, all these traditional challenges make carefree yokels of us all, as well as creating a feeling of well-being and increasing the profits.

The regular sales stalls create the rural atmosphere almost without trying. Country cooking should be in evidence, and preferably have a local, regional flavour; preserves, needlework – a few items decorated with buttercups and daisies for good measure; plants, fruit and vegetables; boxes of chickens' and ducks' eggs spread out on straw matting; dried flowers made up into bunches and others arranged in baskets; posies of garden flowers; see-through envelopes of pressed flowers; all these make lovely souvenirs to take home. Sales girls wearing daisy headbands and carrying a selection of goods in baskets – the 'Won't you buy my pretty flowers?' touch – make a good newspaper photograph.

Refreshments at a country fair can be delightfully and suitably simple, and will no doubt include ploughmen's lunches of wholemeal bread, cheese and pickles; traditional home-baked items such as slices of gingerbread, caraway cake, cherry cake and flapjacks; fairy cakes iced in yellow and white; tea, soft drinks, beer and firkin or two of cider (yes, you will need a licence: see page 103).

A Stars and Stripes Fête, with trans-Atlantic fun for everyone, would be a highlight of anyone's autumn calendar. The big event at one such function I went to was an aerobatic display by an American jet fighter, which flew in from Germany specially; but then it was a very big event indeed, in aid of the St John Ambulance Brigade.

You need to put your thinking cap on for a personality to open such a fête. An American actor or actress playing in a theatre nearby, the head of a manufacturing company or other big employer locally, the commanding officer from a USAF air base, a member of a baseball or American football team suitably padded up – any of these would probably be pleased to do the patriotic honours. And to honour the guest, and deck the place out in the spirit of the occasion, hang out red, white and blue bunting, dress the stalls in these compelling colours and decorate a few with small stars and stripes flags (available cheaply by the dozen from novelty shops).

If you can locate a big-car freak, there is a mint of money to be made if he will offer rides around the field in an old Cadillac: a pink one would be fun. And for the young at heart there could be wagon rides across the prairie in a converted pony and trap (to the tune of 'Surrey with a fringe on top', perhaps). These are just the vehicles to parade around the town a week or two before the event, with stars-and-stripes flags a-fluttering, alerting all and sundry to the coming Yankee invasion.

Capture the children's imagination – and their parents' attention – with the chance of a lifetime, an invitation to take part, for a small consideration, in a real-live pony 'rodeo' (or donkey equivalent). Every rider borrows a 10-gallon hat, and some will come ready dressed for the part, complete with lasso, to take their places in the cowboy-and-his-girl fancy-dress parade.

There may be a local school of dance that would put on a display of square-dancing, with checked skirts a-swirling, and get the customers' feet tapping. And perhaps a similar institution could muster a team of drum majorettes to swing jauntily through the proceedings. Our local town has an artistic roller dance club and the girls have put on some scintillating baton-waving displays in aid of the RSPCA. This would be just the thing to give a stars-and-stripes flavour. Or you might locate one of those tough-guy roller-skating acrobats to go through his breathtaking routine. For these special features, rope off a small area, provide seating and charge a small separate admission fee.

Crack shots and big-shots alike are always drawn to rifle ranges and ten-green-bottle stalls – shoot them all down and you get a bottle with something in it. The marksmanship stalls look even more authentic if you can rig up stable doors, the kind that macho sheriffs burst through as they give awkward customers 'two minutes to get outa town'.

A delightfully folksy attraction that will have them

queuing in the aisles is an old-fashioned cake-walk. You have a record player, the older and more creaky the better, playing Scott Joplin-type music, and a large circle marked out on the ground with numbered places. Then it is like musical chairs: everyone walks around the circle and, when the crackling old music-machine grinds to a halt, rushes frantically to stand on a stopping stone or mat; one of these is removed after each circuit until at the end there is only one left. The winner walks off with a cake, one of many kindly donated by ladies on the food committee.

A fête that recalls a far-away place is an ideal venue at which to launch a balloon race competition. You can buy shining metallic foil balloons with strong, welded seams fit to withstand the fiercest northerly winds, and race-cards with tear-off authorization slips. (For the gas and inflating equipment contact your nearest branch of the British Oxygen Company.) Invite customers to launch their balloons, cross their fingers and see whose is first across to the Big Apple (or some other destination beyond the immediate vicinity of the fête). When you can announce the winner, be sure to tell the local paper. It might like to feature a photograph of the prize presentation. This will be some time after the fête, of course, and useful longer-term publicity for your cause.

Shopping at a Stars and Stripes function is a free and easy affair, but in fairness you should warn patrons to bring a large basket to hold all those goodies from the USA: angel cakes, chiffon pies, apple pies just-like-Mom-used-to-make, jams and jellies, star-shaped cookies and striped candies. Then there will be homespun stalls of gingham gifts, from frilly pillowcases and aprons to rag dolls and cotton roses, needlework pictures and samplers, and miniature toys of all kinds. The Americans are heavily into miniatures, too, and it is a craze that is fast catching on elsewhere: doll's-house furniture, tiny animals, tree decorations – the smaller the better.

The food on such a trans-Atlantic jaunt chooses itself: barbecued chicken, 'franks', hamburgers (don't forget the ketchup) in buns, and cheesecake. People out to enjoy themselves can never resist these foods, which can all be eaten with the fingers.

Christmas comes but once a year, which is just as well,

given the time it takes to organize a full-day, full-scale bazaar and sale of work. Not only that, you have to book up Santa Claus well in advance to drive round town in a decorated lorry and saunter through the shopping precinct handing out leaflets and balloons printed with the date and place of the event.

On the day of the fair he has a place of honour on the stage, and two assistants to help him run the lucky dip, hand out more balloons (they say 'Merry Christmas' this time), distribute presents from under the tree and chat about life back home in the grotto and feeding the reindeer. No, of course he does not charge for the presents. Parents pre-select the main ones from a list carried by one of Santa's nieces circulating in the hall and buy tickets, and the children just hand Father Christmas a number. He needs even more help than that, in fact: a squad of people with lots of puff (or balloon pumps) to blow up the balloons, and others who prefer to spend a companionable afternoon wrapping up toy trumpets, pencil sets and puzzles, books and boxes of crayons.

There will be a big, bumper, fantastic, fabulous Christmas draw that has been going on for months, and another of Santa's nieces will do a brisk trade in selling last-minute tickets in front of a groaning board displaying all the prizes. No one wants to stop to fill in a book of counterfoils – they might miss a bargain on the cake stall – and so two people, working in shifts to avoid getting writer's cramp, will be kept busy filling in the ones below from the details supplied on the top.

The newspaper advertisements will have listed some of the main stalls and, just as in the January sales, people will make a dash for their favourites as soon as the doors are opened on the stroke of ten. You can never tell which stall will attract the most early-birds, but, at least for this initial onslaught, every one will have its 'minder' patrolling from side to side in case there is any sleight of hand.

Old hands at the business know – or will soon learn from experience – that some stalls regularly sell out in record time. Sponge sandwiches, chocolate layers, gingerbread, date slices, cinnamon buns, iced Christmas cakes – everything will disappear from the cake stall like some speeded-up clip of an old film. The meat-pie-and-pâté stall and the Christmas-pudding-and-mince-pie stall will both need restocking at two- or three-hourly intervals, otherwise there will be only bare white tablecloths and apologetic salesladies to greet afternoon shoppers.

Other stalls will keep going at a steady pace through the day. Bright red felt stockings and stacks of stocking-fillers; tree decorations; gifts; produce; groceries; the holly and the ivy (and any other evergreenery that comes to hand); meat and game, and toys.

The toy stall finances itself in an interesting way, by holding Bring-a-Toy coffee mornings throughout the year. For these, you do not pay to come in; you drop a rag doll, finger puppet or bag of marbles into an Ali Baba basket in the porch, then the proceeds of the bring-and-buy table and the inevitable raffle go towards buying toys or the materials for making them at generously favourable prices.

The kitchen at the back of the hall should provide a running buffet of cheese, pâté and ham rolls, mince pies, cakes and sausage rolls (all home-made, thanks to the invention of the home freezer), tea, coffee and soft drinks.

It is such a 'hard sell', a bonanza bazaar like this, that few halls are big enough to allow room for side-shows as well. However, if the press cannot be afforded the opportunity to photograph the guest of honour razing a pile of skittles to the ground, let them show him plunging elbow deep into the bran tub, or buying a bunch of mistletoe.

If you invite a personality or a politician (they are not necessarily the same animal!) to open the event, draw the raffle and generally mingle with the crowds, be sure to detail someone to act as host or hostess. Write a week or two before the event to confirm all the arrangements; check the travel details; meet the guest at the station, if necessary; point out where the cloakroom is; introduce him or her to the committee officers and helpers; make sure the chairman has the biographical notes he needs to introduce the speaker properly; offer the guest a drink and refreshments; provide an umbrella and, if appropriate, organize a posy or spray of flowers to be presented as a token of appreciation. It is all so obvious, but I bet we have all been at functions where the speaker is the only person in the room without a cup of tea, and no one realizes until afterwards that she did not come by car.

A successful fête of any kind is a masterpiece of organization, and only feasible if it is in the hands of a good delegator. The organization of the venue; the general theme; the advertising and publicity; the building, repairing and setting up of stalls; provision of hired seating and other equipment; provision of loos (portable ones if need be); lighting, music and public address system, if any; and refreshments: all are separate areas of responsibility and should be taken over by specialists. It may be the chairman who negotiates for the hall, field or garden, checks on car parking, informs the police and offers the venue for inspection to comply with the fire regulations; the committee decides on the theme. The publicity officer takes it from there, consulting with others in the selection of an overall colour theme; designs the handbills, banners, organizes decorated floats, newspaper advertisements, editorial features, photographs and so forth. A well-disposed builder or handyman recruits and takes charge of the stall squad and organizes collection of any additional seating and tables that may be required. (People like to rest their feet for a while every now and then, and may be charged extra for doing so!) Someone who fully understands the difference between 'live' and 'earth' and preferably has ready access to equipment takes charge of all things electric; he works closely with, and only with the full permission of, the hall caretaker, owner of the field or whatever. An ex-army cook, anyone who has helped with school meals or someone who is completely unflappable sets up a catering and serving team for the running buffet. If he or she is slightly on the fringe of the organization, so much the better. You cannot have the refreshments organizer and the various stallholders trying to tap the same willing sources for puff-pastry sausage rolls.

Each stall or compatible group of stalls should have its own organizer who will get together the necessary manpower (up to a year ahead in some cases) to knit and sew and make and bake the stock; dress the stall; arrange and price the sale goods; and man the stall on a rota system on the day.

The treasurer comes round just before the 'off' with a

cash float for each stallholder, including adequate small change, a receipt book or slip and a paying-in book. He comes again and again throughout the proceedings to collect large denominations of notes, sign for them and, if appropriate, pay them into the on-site bank. Large sums of cash sitting in plastic boxes on exposed expanses of table are at risk.

Pricing can be dicey, because of the inevitable clash of interests. Your job is to make as much money as possible for the cause, and it is tempting to price things on the high side, bearing in mind that food is mostly made with the best of wholesome ingredients (without additives), and giftware and the like will often be hand-made. But there is no justice in this world; customers largely expect to get a bargain, and to pay well below current retail prices.

Make a list of the main types of items you have on sale – cauliflowers, cakes, chutneys – and price them in the shops and market the week before, or even on the morning of the sale. Pitch your prices just below those of your professional competitors – you want satisfied customers, not just customers – and put another 5 pence on the swings and roundabouts, or put an extra effort into selling draw tickets. (A lot more is said about pitching sale prices just right in the chapter entitled 'Sales Pitch'.)

Ladies and gentlemen, the debate on fêtes has only just begun. Just remember that fêtes and fantasies are very closely linked, for all fêtes are flights of fancy. Conjure up the illusion of summer in the country, of far-away places – America, the Orient, the Continent, Hawaii – or a peep into Santa's toy factory, and a good time will be had by all, organizers and customers alike.

CHAPTER 4

Games of chance

The late Joyce Grenfell used to perform a sketch in which she took on the persona of an optimistic ticket-holder during the draw for raffle prizes. She had set her heart on winning the first prize, a holiday for two in the sun. The moment arrived. The chairman called out her name. Great excitement! She had won! But when she went up to claim her prize it was not the tickets to a far-away holiday paradise. Someone else had won those. She had won a 'lovely wabbit', real but dead, which was handed to her on a piece of string. To make matters worse the wabbit wasn't even ready for the pot: he still had his fur coat on. The lucky winner didn't like this. At all. So on the way home, on impulse, she posted the offending unconsolation prize through the open window of a parked car.

The warning implicit in this cautionary tale may well strike a chord with some fund-raisers. None the less, it is true to say that almost everyone loves a gamble and is thrilled to win a prize, no matter what it is. The winning seems to count for more than the prize itself, and even people who frown upon gaming proper look upon the price of a few raffle tickets as a donation to the cause (almost 75 per cent of the adult population of Britain buys the occasional raffle ticket, each year, according to one recent survey). The excitement, applause and shouts of 'Fix!', 'Fiddle!' and 'Draw again!' when someone jumps up to receive a prize, be it shampoo or champagne, shows that we are all children at heart. In this game of chance, if your number comes up, suddenly it feels like Christmas and birthday rolled into one.

Raffles, tombolas, guessing games, 'horse-racing', they all have their ardent devotees. Indeed, it is difficult to envisage a fund-raising function without at least one such attraction. Firstly, they raise extra cash, and secondly they give the participants pleasure: the perfect combination.

Indeed, *not* holding a draw can cause great disappointment. We once took a group of elderly people on a mystery coach trip, finishing up with tea in a country garden. We had raised the money from a coffee morning and other events, but it had not occurred to us to organize a raffle for the outing itself. The idea was to give the folk a good time, not to ask them to put their hands in their pockets. Then, on the way home, one lively old lady asked when the tickets were coming round. As soon as she heard that they were not, she took matters in hand herself. Bits of paper torn off the tops of newspapers and numbered served as tickets, and were vigorously shaken up in a cap. The prizes were a few souvenir items the passengers had bought on the outing, and which they gladly sacrificed in this sudden emergency: a strip of half-a-dozen pansy plants, a bar of National Trust soap and a pot of home-made jam were received by the three winners with transports of delight. The raffle made their day. Another time, we will know!

You do have to observe certain rules and regulations if you are organizing a raffle, or any other game of chance for that matter, otherwise you could find yourself falling foul of the law. A raffle which takes place at a function at which all the tickets are sold and the prizes drawn is defined as a 'small lottery'. These are fairly straightforward: the law assumes that the attraction of the raffle is ancillary to the main event – in other words, that people would go on the coach outing, attend the fête or buy tickets for the supper party even if there were *not* a raffle, and that the lottery is just the profitable icing on the cake.

You may not, of course, use any of the takings for private gain, but you may use up to £50 to buy the prizes, pay for any printing of tickets or subsidize the cost of the hall, entertainment or refreshments. On the subject of refreshments, if you have a justice's 'off' licence or an 'Occasional Permission' to serve alcohol during the event, it is all right to offer spirits, wine (including home-made wine, which is subject to the same regulations) and other alcohol as prizes: the overall legal requirements are already satisfied. If no such permission has been requested, and granted, that means no alcoholic prizes may be offered. (Beware: this is a trap into which the organizers of many a vicar's tea-party have fallen.) Moreover you may not, in a small lottery, offer cash prizes, or vouchers that are exchangeable for cash. By all means ask a butcher or a hairdresser for a voucher that can be used in his or her shop, but do not ask the retailer to clip a £5 note to one of his billheads and put it in an envelope as a mystery prize.

Leaving the law aside for a moment, there cannot be many people who would support an event simply because it was going to include a raffle; but there is no denying that the chance of a flutter can be a magnetic added attraction. Try it. When you are organizing a fête, put a great big teddy bear on the front of the toy stall, an attractively arranged box or basket of fruit well to the fore of the produce table and a celebration gâteau as the centrepiece on the cake stall. Have someone on hand selling raffle tickets for these special prizes at 10 or 20 pence a time. People will swarm towards them like bees round a honey-pot, jostle with one another to buy tickets and then have a look to see what else is on the stalls.

If the bazaar or fête runs for more than one day, as it might for a week-long village festival, raffles may be run right through the event, as long as the winning tickets are drawn and the winners announced before the end. There is always a hard core of people who will turn up specially, at 4.30 on the final afternoon, to see fair play – and, they hope, to walk off with a prize – even when it has been raining solidly for two-and-a-half days and everyone is soaking wet.

There is quite a bit of financial wizardry involved in running a raffle so that you can be sure to maximize the profit potential. The skill comes in striking the right balance between the value of the prizes and the amount you are likely to collect from the sale of tickets. There is nothing more depressing, from the treasurer's point of view, than to see the lucky winners walk jauntily off with prizes worth well over £40, only to tip out the moneybags and find that the takings barely top the £30 mark. For one thing, no one can reasonably expect the value of the prizes to exceed the amount collectively staked to win them – gambling isn't like that. And for another, it is somewhat dispiriting for the kind folk who donated the prizes, confidently supposing they were contributing towards a good profit, if the outcome is a deficit. If this topsy-turvy ratio ever does occur, it will be due to plain bad management, and rapping over the knuckles will be in order.

The first essential in a raffle is to make a guesstimate of how much money you might reasonably hope to take on the raffle. This is not quite the 'How long is a piece of string?' question it may seem, and it is crucial to make the calculation with resonable accuracy. It is no good getting in a galaxy of glittering prizes and optimistically assuming that you will more than cover the cost on the night. Of course people will go out to a function prepared to spend generously if it is in a good cause; and if the ticket sellers do their job, spend generously they will. But everybody has a limit, and it is also important to keep your expectations in proportion. If people are paying for a couple of glasses of wine and a plate of cheese straws to raise funds to resurface the school drive, not many of them are going to give you a £10 note and tell you to keep the change. Equally, if they are hell-bent on a good night out at a ritzy venue – and especially if there is an element of keeping up with the Joneses – then the sky could well be the limit.

Whoever volunteers for the job of looking after the raffle (or tombola, for that matter) should be kept closely in touch with other aspects of the organization. She should be one of the first to know how many tickets have been sold or, if the event is open to the general public, how wide the publicity net has been spread and roughly how many people the organizers hope to attract. If this is an annual event or follows fairly closely on the lines of one that has been held before, now is the time to look up the records of the last occasion to check the attendance figures and see how the raffle fared. While the books are open, it is worth looking to see who was generous enough to donate the prizes, too.

It is hard to generalize, even harder to be specific, on the subject of possible raffle proceeds. Accuracy is in any case impossible, owing to the human element and the rate of inflation, among other influences. However, in my own experience, people wandering from stall to stall at a bazaar or fête, who have not paid to come in and are not necessarily devoted to the cause in question, might be expected to spend around the cost of two popular daily newspapers on raffle tickets – maybe more if one of the prizes is a cuddly teddy bear and their children plead sufficiently. People out to enjoy themselves at a barbecue, lunch or supper party might spend something like one-fifth to one-quarter of the ticket price per couple. If each ticket costs £5 you would be doing well to sell on average £1's-worth of tickets between two people. There will always be one or two men who are feeling on top of the world and will be prepared to dig deeper into their pockets. But there will be others who have stretched themselves to come at all. So it evens out.

The ratio of prize value to ticket money is a matter of choice – some might say almost of conscience. Who can say what is right? If you have been lucky enough to have all the prizes donated, you might think that a prize value of about one-quarter of the takings estimate would be about right, going down to one-fifth, say, if by some mischance all the prizes have to be bought and paid for. You may think this is either wildly over-generous or diabolically mean: in that case let the committee decide.

People are funny about prizes. They take it for granted that there will be a raffle at a fund-raising function and delve into their handbags or pockets as soon as someone approaches with a cheerful sales smile and a book of tickets. But as to the prizes themselves, scarcely a soul ever seems to ask what they are or to take the trouble to go and see them on display. Personally, I look on bottles of booze, boxes of chocolates, biscuits and stationery, cosmetics and soaps as fairly standard stuff: pleasant to win, certainly, but not earth-shattering.

It is rather fun, from everyone's point of view, to have at least one prize that is more of a talking point, something people do not take for granted. There was quite a stampede to buy tickets at a barn dance I went to recently. One of the committee owns a twin-seater plane and had offered to take the first-prize winner for a trip around – or rather above – the local villages. The chance to take aerial photographs of their own home and to have a peek into the gardens of everybody else's proved a great attraction to punters – and the sales graph almost did a vertical take-off.

If your Member of Parliament is coming to the function, and particularly if it is being held in aid of party funds, he or she might be persuaded to donate a bottle of sherry or a box of chocolate mints with a distinctive dark green and white House of Commons label – something you do not come across every day. On very special occasions an MP might go further and offer dinner for two, or tea on the terrace of the Houses of Parliament: again, something that in the ordinary course of events money cannot buy, and a prize that definitely commands a high premium.

Local tradespeople and national food chains enter into the spirit of prize-giving in all kinds of ways. Shopkeepers might offer to make up a hamper for a Sunday lunch, with a joint of meat, vegetables, fruit, cream and a bottle of wine, or give a voucher for a turkey or a box of groceries. It is fun if the prize-winner can make his or her own choice of groceries, though, and especially in the somewhat unconventional way offered by a group of shops in the north-east: it gave the first-prize winners at four functions raising funds for a heart scanner the chance of a 1½-minute 'dash-and-grab' raid. For a prize like this you would first have to go to the store to do a 'recce', and also to check where the shopping trolleys are and the fastest route to the counter of your choice (alcohol and tobacco are normally excluded from such exploits). The truly dedicated might want to go to keep-fit classes for a week or two beforehand to limber up. Such a prize gives the ticket sellers an unusual line of patter, puts up the sales and almost guarantees publicity for both the fund-raising event and the store in the following week's newspaper, if not on television.

I do not know whether anyone has ever written a sales manual, raffle-ticket sellers for the use of. Someone probably has; after all, there are sales manuals for just about everything else. If there *were* such a handbook, it might start by advising readers to let people get inside the doors first before bombarding them with tickets and asking them for money. Not long ago I went to a very stylish buffet supper party in an old rectory. Just as the guests had succeeded in fumbling their way in the pitch dark to the top of the steps, and before they had had the chance to shuffle out of their coats or put their scarves in their pockets, they were pounced on by three eager beavers selling raffle tickets. The chilly response they received from just about everyone, together with an almost unprecedented sales resistance throughout the rest of the evening, was no more than they deserved. Next in everyman's guide to coaxing money out of visitors, I suppose, would come the old trick of having at least two books in circulation, with different-coloured tickets. That gives the vendors on sales drive number 2 the chance to say, 'Ah yes, but you haven't had any of *mine*. The pink ones.' You wouldn't think people would still fall for it, but luckily they do. If the occasion includes a lunch or supper, there is a lot to be said for going round with tickets for the final time once people have enjoyed their meal. I would like to have a new typewriter ribbon for every time someone has said, 'You've all looked after us so well, I will just have one more strip.'

Selling tickets at 50 pence each, or 50 pence for a strip of five: which is it to be? Apart from the cost of the tickets themselves, which is minimal, there is virtually no difference. People will spend precisely the same amount of money, but will tend to think that with a strip of five tickets in their hands they are getting more chances. They are not, of course, because assuming that no one would actually accept more than one prize, the ratio of chances to prizes is exactly the same. But we are in the illusion business here, so give them five for their money.

To prevent a bottleneck at the end of the proceedings, have some people on hand ready to start folding the tickets in batches as they are sold. To save time, tear out a complete strip of five, fold it lengthways once, and then again, to make a long, very thin strip; tear off the tickets at the four perforations, and they will all be neatly folded. This is infinitely quicker than tearing off and folding each one.

The long arm of the law takes slightly more interest in the kind of raffle for which the tickets are sold in advance of the event, as they often are for a grand Christmas draw, or one which is to be the highlight of a fête or festival. In such cases the raffle has to be defined as a 'society lottery', and the organizing society must be registered with the local authority. Once this is done, the tickets – which may not cost more than 50 pence each – can be sold from door to door (though not in the course of business: you may not ask the insurance man to sell a few for you on his rounds), through the post or in any other way. Also, the total ticket value must currently not exceed £10,000. Over that limit, details of the scheme must be submitted to the gaming board as well. You must show the name and address of the promoter and the registering authority on the tickets – any local printer will know the rules by heart – and it pays you, in terms of sales, to list the most attractive prizes.

Having put your lottery on a firm legal footing, how do you sell the most tickets? Everyone on the committee, everyone who has made a donation in the past, given prizes or shown an interest in the cause in any way should be asked to take a few books to sell. Pubs and clubs are often extremely helpful. The main thing is to impress on people that with just a bit of combined effort, there is real money in this venture. Make one person, or a small group, responsible for listing who has which ticket numbers. Tick off each book when the counterfoils are returned with the money, and phone round a few days in advance of the draw to remind latecomers.

I once had an embarrassing stroke of luck at one of those draws which seems to go on for most of the autumn and culminates at the end of the Christmas market. I had been selling tickets with the line that the first prize of £100 was really something. And then, standing at the back of the hall and with nothing, I swear, up my sleeve, I won it. Quite an advance on Joyce Grenfell's lovely rabbit! I had double glazing fitted to a couple of windows, as a lasting reminder that gambling does pay.

The third category of lottery, according to the legal definition, is a 'private lottery'. These may be organized only for an individual society, or group of people who live or work together – a social club, old people's home and so forth. The promoter must be one of that group, and must be authorized by the committee, governing body or manager to hold the raffle, and the whole proceeds (after the deduction of expenses) must go to the group. Tickets must all be sold at the same price – you may not offer them at 10 pence individually but 50 pence for six – and their sale must be confined to the specified premises; there may be no advertising, no hawking round door-to-door, and no mailing of tickets. Private lotteries are clearly not the biggest money-spinners on earth, but they can raise useful funds for a cause. It is amazing how often members of a workers' club or suchlike will, on the spur of the moment, decide to do their bit for a good cause.

When, finally, the draw is announced, the tickets are first jumbled up in a hat, shopping basket or other container. If you have a guest of honour, this could be the time for the chairman to say a few complimentary words, thanking him for so generously giving up his time and joining other guests in what he hopes has been a pleasant occasion. And then the guest or other designate will draw out the tickets, eyes a-sparkle, as if he is performing the ceremony for the very first time, call out the names, present the prizes as each recipient comes forward, and perhaps sing a few words of praise about the organizers and the good work they are doing. For many people, the draw may well be the highlight of the occasion. However, lines of winners pushing back their chairs and walking the length of the hall for yet another bar of soap or packet of envelopes can be a social disaster and will kill conversation stone dead. A few good prizes that are really worthy of appreciation are likely to be the best bet.

If it should happen that people respond so generously to the call that they continue to arrive all day long, bringing more and more prizes for the raffle, you should make a mental note to run a tombola instead next time – you need far more prizes for that, and it has the potential to make you a far higher profit. Then you take out a couple of the gifts to use as star attractions, and explain to your best friends among the donors that you are putting by several of the other items for the next event: frankly, you can consider yourself very lucky to have such a problem.

Once people are in the party mood there is no holding them when it comes to games of chance and guessing games. Children love to go round a fête or bazaar with a prettily dressed doll asking people to guess her name. You can write all the suggestions down on a list, but what happens if no one gets it right, or several people have the same idea? It is easier to make a long list of names and ask people to sign their own name against one. Put the winning choice – Amanda, Jane or whatever – and a couple of reserves (in case some names on the list have no takers) into an envelope and seal it. Then ask one of the children to announce the winner and present the prize.

How many beans in the jar? How many matches in the large box? How many sweets in the tin? Guess the weight of the cake. How many pounds have these simple competitions raised over the decades? How many hours of fun have these familiar games given fund-raisers over the years? Quite a few, and they are no doubt good for a few more yet. What is more, they can all be used as a blueprint for other notions based on similar themes.

On one of our committees we have a Paddington Bear freak, and whenever she is asked to organize a sideshow, you can bet your bottom dollar, if you have not already spent it on the raffle, that somewhere in the thick of it there will be a snout-nosed furry personage with a stout pair of wellingtons and a floppy felt hat (under which he keeps his bacon sandwiches, of course).

Once we have judged that one prize more will not make a scrap of difference to the raffle takings, and we have a captive audience at something like a supper party, off we go with the silly games. One year we had a large whisky bottle partly filled with cold tea. The dodge was to guess how many teaspoons (or 5-ml spoons, for the metricated) Paddington's Great Aunt Lucy had resorted to as medicinal compound. (The publican who was running the bar was barred from entering.) Just going round the tables while people were having their coffee and posing this simple conundrum raised over £40 from about 100 guests – money which certainly would not have been added to the raffle takings.

Another time the large model bear himself, suitably spruced up for the occasion, was toted round for people to guess his weight. It was quite something to see the farmers jumping him up and down on their shoulders, comparing his weight with that of a new-born piglet. Mothers did the same thing, trying to work out the toy bear's weight in relation to that of their last baby at birth. Bears being not a lot like either young pigs or bouncing babies, amazingly nobody guessed to within a couple of pounds.

Then there was our version of 'X marks the spot', with a large poster of our hero and, in the corner, a badge depicting him falling off a ladder with a pot of paint. All you had to do was to write your name on a paper flag and stick it in the poster where you thought Paddington would pin his badge. It was in his hat, actually, and people contributed about another £45 to our funds in their efforts to work this out.

When there is a bottle of scotch or some other nectar to spare, you used to be able to make a handy extra profit by asking people to sign their name on a £1 note and put it in a jar. Now you have to ask them to sign identical slips of paper, and put in a coin instead. If you would like to offer your guests specially favourable odds, you can limit the number of entries each time to, say, ten or twelve. You will need more prizes to go round, and will almost certainly make less profit, but it is still a good money-spinner.

On the subject of money-spinning, the whirr of the tombola drum, rotating like an old-fashioned ice-cream churn, holds a fatal fascination for lots of folk. If you are organizing a long-running function such as a fête or bazaar, or have a fairly large audience with time on its hands – a buffet supper with a minimal number of speeches, for example – a tombola can be just the ticket. Much the same rules and regulations apply as for a small lottery: sell the tickets only at the event, distribute the prizes then and there (you would be doing that anyway), have alcohol as prizes only if you have the appropriate licence, and do not offer cash.

Once you are on the fund-raising merry-go-round you will find that there is always someone who specializes in pretty well whatever you happen to have in mind, including tombolas. Someone in our village just loves organizing them and will take over the reins for any function, just for the asking. Her mind works like a computer on matters like the value of prizes to takings ratio and the ratio of prizes to tickets. Ask around. If you see a tombola stall at someone else's function, find out who organized it and ask if she, or he, would be prepared to do the same for you. Ask members of other committees. As always, it is not *what* you know, but *who* you know. And if, after all that, you do not come across anyone who is a natural for the job, it is not that difficult to organize for yourself anyway. Although tombolas require marginally more mathematics than pinning a badge on a Paddington Bear poster, they are potentially much more profitable.

The principle of a tombola is the exact reverse of a raffle. In a raffle of any kind, the chosen dignitary closes his eyes, stirs the tickets around ostentatiously, picks out one and announces the winning number. In a tombola, the punters pick out their own tickets. So you must not fall into the trap of having all the prizes labelled with blue tickets, and lots of white ones in the box with no corresponding goodies. People are apt to notice! For the same reason it really is worth begging, borrowing or making a simple drum with an aperture. It creates a stir and seems more legal.

You need a good nucleus of 'top' prizes, the kind of items that will make people spend and spend until they do win them. The best I ever had in this regard was a set of top-quality non-stick pans in the most fashionable shade of pale grey, beautifully done up in a see-through box. Luckily this prize was still going strong almost at the end of the proceedings and probably generated more interest than the rest of the stock put together. The lady who won it could have bought a set in the hardware shop next door for two-thirds of what those pans cost her, but she did not seem to mind.

Equally important, you need masses of smaller prizes, ones which are fun to win but not ultimately satisfying. People will come back to their table with a bottle of sauce and a pair of tights, have another drink and then go back to the stall, determined to have a go for the champagne.

Some tombolas are organized so that every ticket wins a prize of some kind, which is fine if you can charge a really good price for the tickets and most of the prizes have been donated. We had a lady on one of our committees who made it virtually her life's work to collect tombola prizes for an annual event. She did not want to know about ratios, prices or organization. Her job was the prizes. In and out of the shops she went, smiling cheerily and full of enthusiasm for the cause, and out she would come with a handbag, a kitchen stool, a box of wine glasses, a pack of playing cards, a pair of pillow cases, a couple of children's books, and vouchers galore. It was just as well that she had a big spare room in which to keep them all.

It really is not necessary to run the tombola on 'every one a winner' lines; a ratio of one winning ticket in five is generally acceptable. This means that you stick one-half of all the cloakroom tickets ending in zero and five on to the prizes; scrap all the in-between halves, the twos, threes and so on, and put all the counterfoils into the drum. It is a job to be done quietly, when you can concentrate properly. Pity the red-faced stallholder who has a customer gleefully holding out a something-five ticket, only to find that there is no corresponding prize. (It is as well to have a few prizes in reserve, under the table, in case this ever does happen. Goodwill is a commodity you cannot afford to squander.)

Bottle stalls are organized in just the same way, and not all the bottles need to come from the off-licence. It is fun to have tiny sample bottles of perfume, cologne, cosmetics, plant fertilizer, sauce, flavourings, preserves, ink, poster paints, even junk-stall ginger beer bottles; the more variety the merrier.

Presentation is of great importance to a tombola – it is the sales stall *par excellence* and should act like a magnet from quite some distance. Ask around to see if anyone has a set of staging, or make steps by arranging boxes in diminishing heights. Cover the stall neatly, have a massive banner above it, and do everything you possibly can to make the stall itself – let alone the helpers – shout, 'Roll up, roll up!' Important: no one likes to mistrust anyone at an all-pals-together event, but prizes have been known to disappear while the winning tickets were still in the drum, so it is best to fence off the stall and have all those enticements just out of arm's reach.

As a variation on putting folded tickets in a drum or other container, there is the good old-fashioned straw stall. You select your winning tickets in just the same way, then roll up all the counterfoils – winners and no-gos – and push each one into the end of a straw. This is all very well if you have hordes of helpers longing to sit around for hours straw-filling, but a refinement that a busy committee is likely to find tiresome.

The horse-racing game is another fund-raising ploy based on gambling. But be warned. One of the worst messes I ever got into, trying to raise money for a worthy cause, was heralded by two policemen turning up on our front doorstep at half-past six one Saturday evening. Sorry, they said, but we couldn't hold the horse-racing event in the town hall as planned that evening: in one hour and a half from then, to be exact! Since then I have been, perhaps understandably, decidedly off these events. Though maybe that is a bit unfair.

For horse-racing, you buy a complete package from an agency. You receive a film of the whole proceedings, showing horses and riders parading round the paddock, so that guests can assess form with as much accuracy, and just about as much chance of winning, as if they were actually there on the race course. The horses are given numbers and these are used all through the filmed races, the American commentary getting more and more hectic as each one bolts to a climax. You also get tote cards and all those bits and pieces they have in betting shops, so that the evening is high on authenticity. In advance of the event, someone gives the horses jokey names that will sell them like hot tips to people in the audience: number 4 in the first race might be Computer Colin, number 8 Bookworm Bill, others might be Phil the Farmer, Pretty Polly, Blonde Bombshell and so forth. The evening starts with someone acting as auctioneer and 'selling' the horses. Now a select – and, it is to be hoped, generous – few in the audience have a special interest in the races. Throughout the evening, as each filmed race is run, winnings are collected, bets placed on the next, and so on, excitement and money mounting all the while.

If you have the right kind of environment, and the right kind of clientele, you can sweep the board, in fund-raising terms. One of these racing events held locally attracted over 200 people, raised £200 on the sale of the horses and brought in a net profit of £1,200.

If the idea appeals to you, do take every precaution. It seems to me that this game is a lot more chancy than most. You can only hold a horse-racing event between members of a private club or organization; you must not advertise it in any way; and it is subject to various other regulations, too. You would be well advised to check first with your local police before launching such a function. The policemen on my doorstep were full of apologies, but because one invitation had slipped through the club network and been passed on to a racing fanatic who was not a member, and someone had reported the fact, our big race was off. The tote never opened its shutters and members of the committee spent the worst part of the evening at the doors of the town hall, explaining to guests what had happened.

Still, the pub next door did a good trade. It's an ill wind . . .

CHAPTER 5

How much am I bid?

'Start me off, someone. Five pounds? Two pounds? One pound, then? Come on, we've got to make a start somewhere. One pound – lady in the front row!'

No matter what is on offer, whether it is the dusty contents of an old lady's attic or a collection of fine wines donated over a period of months, once the sale starts, the excitement mounts, an element of competition creeps in and within a short space of time 'You, sir' in the duffle coat at the back of the room is going all out to beat 'You, madam' with the poodle in the front row. After a few moments of leapfrogging prices, be they in pence or pounds, the gavel descends. Lot number 1 has found a home.

Auctions are one of the most rewarding ways of raising money, the perfect charity matchmakers. What they do is provide a forum to bring together items that somebody somewhere does not want any more, or is at least prepared to part with in aid of a good cause, and a collection of people who, once the sale gets under way and they get into the mood, are prepared to vie with each other to buy those very same things. It goes without saying that, as for all forms of matchmaking, creating the perfect match between the sale items and the audience is one of the many challenges of putting on a successful auction.

What you should know, however, right from the start, is that successful auctions do not happen by accident. The occasion of the sale represents only the tip of the iceberg. In fact, most of the work is done well before it, in some cases months beforehand.

First of all, if you are going to organize an auction, it is important that you should convey accurately to both donors and buyers the scale and type of the sale you are putting on. You will not want people turning up just for the sake of something to do on a rainy Saturday afternoon, with only a few pence in their pockets, if what you have on offer is fine silverware and exquisite china. Equally, you cannot afford to announce a glittering occasion if you are more than likely to be offered items that wouldn't look out of place at a car-boot sale. So it is up to the organizing committee to pitch the sale just right.

The auction itself need not be the sole attraction: sales can be held in conjunction with a lunch, a cheese-and-wine party, a buffet supper or sherry evening – anything to entice people to attend. The advantages of providing drink are not merely convivial. It is a well-proven fact that once the wine is flowing and customers are in a buoyant mood, the sale catalogues wave more frequently, the auctioneer's eye is caught more persistently and the whole event gathers momentum and money.

If yours is an area where auctions occur fairly frequently and you think one more plea for sale goods might fall on stony ground, bear in mind that you can run a sale without a single tangible item (think of all the arm-ache that saves the would-be stewards during the course of the event!). Some of the most exciting and amusing auctions are 'promises sales' where you do not collect items at all, but pledges of service. It is an equally good idea for a housing estate, where people might offer to babysit or mind a child during the day, or a country area, where families with a car might offer shopping trips into town for elderly people or someone with a young child.

These are useful services. Others on offer at a recent cheese-and-wine 'promises' sale held in aid of a boy scouts' group became a little more ambitious and, in some cases, got a little out of hand. For example, a load of farmyard manure, which you could have detected with your nasal organs from several hundred yards away, went for what appeared to be many times its weight in gold; someone with a vintage car raised the princely sum of £180 by offering the passenger seat for the London-to-Brighton Run; a young housewife with a flair for cooking offered to prepare a dinner-party for four, with her husband on hand, pinny at the ready, to wash up afterwards: this raised another £36 for the fund.

And so it went on. Car-washing by the youngsters themselves; video shows or discos for Christmas parties;

a children's cabaret which, going for a song, was snatched up by the secretary of the senior citizens' club; sweaters knitted, any size, any style, bidder to provide the wool – it is amazing what an enormous variety of services may be on offer in any given locality, and an auction is the ideal vehicle for making the most of the resources and swelling the charity kitty at the same time. Equally, it is quite astonishing what some people, caught up in the mood of the occasion, are prepared to pay for those services.

With so many possibilities, the hardest decision you have to make is exactly what type of sale to put on. That executive hurdle over, the next thing to consider is whether to run the auction yourselves or to call in the professionals. The size and type of the sale will serve as a guide. If you are aiming to raise a few pounds for the Brownie outing by selling off a heap of used toys, books and clothes, one of the parents will probably step in and fill the bill adequately. Equally, if you have a large committee and band of helpers who are used to raising money in a number of ways, there is sure to be someone who can take this kind of thing in his or her stride – and, indeed, who will enjoy the challenge. But not everybody would be able, or happy, to run an auction, so never try to force the job on to anyone who claims to be too shy to cope. They know best!

Someone with a flair for amateur dramatics and who is not afraid of making a fool of himself or herself should be able to juggle well enough with all the various elements. These include jollying the audience along when things go slack, moving on quickly when an item 'sticks' (by knocking it down to the 'house' rather than admitting there was no sale) and laughing off the inevitable gaffe which all amateur, and some professional, auctioneers make – such as knocking lot number 111 down to a man who was only scratching his ear (it does happen!). Obviously you want your sale to be as well-run and efficiently managed as possible, but the occasional hiccup is not the end of the world, and as long as the auctioneer does not show acute signs of embarrassment and lose his cool completely, the audience will enter into the spirit of it. In any case, a few light-hearted moments never come amiss on such occasions.

If you are hoping for a collection of highly saleable items and an audience in a fairly serious buying mood – and there is nothing like a charity sale to prick the consciences and the cheque books – then it is well worth considering handing over the job to a firm of professional auctioneers. This does not mean you will have to hand over a percentage of the profits. Most auctioneers will handle a charity sale, even at weekends or in the evenings, without any form of charge: they do it for the good of the cause and the local publicity.

Think about it. Certainly anyone who saw the BBC television programme *In at the Deep End* in which the presenter, Chris Serle, conducted part of a London sale after a crash course in auctioneering will appreciate the complexities of the job. To stand up on the rostrum and keep the whole thing moving along entertainingly and profitably demands great skill and powers of concentration. We had watched Serle, in the early weeks of his training, solemnly chanting at his shaving mirror the leaps and bounds in which the prices rise, hoping to land neatly on any bid already left with the auctioneers. No multiplication tables at school were ever more difficult to learn by heart! After the sale, he was seen jumping down from the rostrum declaring how thankful he was that he did not have to do this for a living.

If a professional auctioneer agrees to handle your sale, he will bring along trained staff to keep the books (and will pay them himself, too), using the double-entry bookkeeping system. He will probably bring one or two assistants to man the doors, too, to ensure that only goods that have been paid for leave the premises. (Yes, theft is a possibility – and losing money destined for your chosen charity is somehow even worse than losing your own.)

In a local community it is almost impossible to avoid clashes or near-misses with function dates, but do remember that there is a limit to the number of times people can turn out their attic, garage or spare room, even in a good cause. If time is on your side, monitor the local papers to see whether a pattern of regular auctions crops up for other fund-raising groups, and ask any contacts you have on those committees. The auctioneer will probably have a good idea, too, of what is going on locally and might be able to steer you away from a date too close to another event.

Where are you going to hold the sale? If you are collecting funds for improvements to the village hall, scouts' hut or sports pavilion, the venue will probably select itself, as long as the building is suitable. Otherwise, you might be able to borrow a barn or outhouse from a local farmer, or you may have to hire a hall or a tent. Check that the building has adequate access – you need good big doors or entrances if you are likely to be selling large pieces of furniture. And, when the time comes, the Fire Officer will want to be sure that there are at least two exits readily accessible throughout the sale as a standard safety precaution.

If you are able to hold the function in a barn or tent on someone's land, and particularly if it is to be one of the 'eat first, buy later' types of sale, then the host – who is presumably well disposed towards your cause – may agree to sign personal letters of invitation. (You provide the letters ready-typed, giving details of the sale and, after agreeing the wording with him, clearly stating the host's support of the charity. He signs them. You despatch them.) Equally irresistible is a letter from a local personality inviting people to come to lunch and participate afterwards in all the fun of the sale. Otherwise, a letter from the president or chairman of your committee, couched in such a way that the recipient feels specially important to be invited, should do the trick.

Whether it is a letter of invitation or a handbill delivered door to door, get your publicity material out in good time. Turning out the gloryhole takes a good deep breath and the right kind of day. People need notice. Sometimes, for charity, the newsagents, free-newspaper distributors or milkmen will agree to deliver handouts to each house on their round. Otherwise, it is a perfect job for youngsters or for someone who feels that a gentle stroll from one letterbox to the next is about the limit of his or her desire to be involved.

Never feel embarrassed about leaning on people in this way. After all, it is not your own personal benevolent fund that you are asking them to support. It is hard for someone to refuse if you say something like, 'Our committee is organizing an auction to raise money for the new wing of the village hall. We're putting on a cold buffet lunch before the sale, offering to collect and deliver sale items, and give lifts to anybody who hasn't got transport. I wonder whether you could possibly get one or two friends together to help deliver the notices to everyone in the area? It would be such a help.' Most people are flattered to be asked for help and like to feel needed, so you are very likely to receive a favourable response.

Whether you opt for a letter or a handbill to announce your sale, set out all the necessary information clearly: the name of the charity; the date, time and place of the sale; the cost of admission if any (it is not usual to make one, unless of course you are serving refreshments); the deadline for delivery of items for sale, and whether you are prepared to collect them (if you want plenty of goods, you'll have to!); the time and duration of the preview (see below); the terms and conditions of sale (see below); the deadline for collecting any unsold items; when you propose to pay out the donors' share of the money raised; whether you are able to offer lifts to people who could not otherwise attend; and lastly (very important), the names, addresses and telephone numbers of people to contact in the event of any queries. If a professional auctioneer is handling the sale for you free of charge, it is a courtesy to mention this on any notice or poster, though you must make it clear by implication that the auctioneer has *not* undertaken to take messages about picking up bed-settees from the next parish at any time convenient to the organizers, as long as it is between 3.30 and 4.15 on the third Friday in the month.

It is important for potential buyers to have the opportunity to view the goods before the sale. Unless you are dealing with a very big or prestigious sale that will attract people from far and wide – in which case one or two days may be needed – a couple of hours before the start is usually long enough for the preview.

Organizations vary in how they handle the 'terms and conditions'. Some charities work on the basis that they keep 25 per cent of the sale price, while the rest goes to the donor. Some keep 50 per cent. Some charities keep more of the profit, some less. And of course a good many donors are only too happy to part with the items, and do not want any of the sale proceeds. So much the better, but if you at least make the gesture and offer donors a share of the takings, you will probably be able to amass more goods for sale. (You will be surprised how many people who say they want their percentage ultimately donate the whole proceeds once the sale is over. They, too, get caught up in the spirit of the thing.)

To have a catalogue of sale items, or not: that is another question. Whenever there are 'quality' items on sale, it is a good idea to have them listed in order of appearance, with a brief description. A professional auctioneer would certainly include this as part of the service he offered. A catalogue makes it much easier for potential buyers to note which lots are of special interest to them and make an assessment of their value. (The auctioneer's job, of course, is to build up the competition to such a pitch that people throw caution to the winds and forget when their ceiling price has been reached.)

A catalogue, however basic, gives you a chance to sell advertising space in advance: local tradesmen will readily appreciate that you will have a captive audience and that people who attend charity auctions buy groceries, have their hair cut, go to pubs, have lawnmowers and washing machines that break down, and buy petrol. Members of the committee can ask their own special contacts well in advance of the event, offering advertising space for a nominal fee. The advertisements need be only a few lines clearly typed and well set out; they could appear, perhaps, on alternate pages, or on the inside of the cover. But preparing all this takes time. If you decide to have a catalogue be sure to add at least one day, preferably two, to the deadline for delivery of items.

It takes time, too, to set all the items out in selling order, arranged around the perimeter of the sale-room (or sale-tent, as the case may be). You cannot leave this until the last minute, tempting though that may be, because in spite of all your pleas and protestations about deadlines, people are likely to arrive with the sale items long after the stated time. What you do is have a 'stop press' section at the end of the catalogue, or even a few unitemized lots to sell at the end. Never refuse any offer of saleable goods.

On the thorny question of unsold items, ask donors *at the time of collection* what their wishes are. If donors want the items back, then specify a deadline for collection. You will find, however, that having made the decision to donate the goods in the first place, many people never want to see them again: more profit for your funds! Organize a local dealer to come and buy 'unsolds' as a job lot – making very sure first, of course, that there are no priceless antiques or first editions among the collection.

Do not forget insurance. It is certainly advisable, for all but the most casual of sales, to have a policy that covers the risks of fire and theft. You may find that the premises are covered by a comprehensive policy. If not, think laterally. Is there someone on your committee, or a local businessman who has shown an interest in the cause, who might cover the cost of the policy as a donation? There is never any harm in asking, and there is no point in depleting the profits when you can get something for nothing.

Unless your sale is a ticket-only affair (as it would be for a supper sale), put posters in prominent places around the locality – ones that are clear enough to be read from a passing car. And consider taking an advertisement in a local paper: every area has 'auction freaks' who will turn up at every sale. Incidentally, many local papers offer a half-price discount for all fund-raising advertisements.

If you are going it alone, without professional help, you will need plenty of volunteers at every stage of the proceedings: two people to receive, enter and number goods as they arrive, two people to assist with the bookkeeping at the sale, at least two sturdy chaps to lift up the items one by one as the lot numbers are called out – unless it is a promises sale, that is – and one or two people to stand security on the door at the end of the proceedings.

To keep track of all the sale items from the word 'go', have sheets of paper already ruled up in five columns before goods start arriving: the first will show a provisional lot number for the item; the second, a description of the item; the third, the name and address of the donor; the fourth, the 'reserve price', if any – the minimum amount for which the donor is prepared to let it go; the fifth should record the percentage of the sale price the donor wishes to receive, if any. If your sale is to be on the 'anything goes' type, you can list a fox-fur tippet next to a kitchen stool, next to a pair of skates, followed by a pile of comics, and so on, and the first 'admission number' can stand. If not, and the items are to be grouped in sections, all furniture together, all pictures together and so on, then you will need to re-number them – and to be very careful in so doing.

White cloakroom (or raffle) tickets are clear and simple for numbering the items. Attach one half firmly to the sale item with sticky tape. Make a chronological list, for the auctioneer and the bookkeepers, or clerks, and for the catalogue if there is to be one. And check, check and check again that the items, their lot numbers and the lists match up. On paper, at least, this sounds like a relatively straightforward job – but it is surprising how often it goes wrong, to the embarrassment of helpers and auctioneer alike.

Not so long ago I was at a sale in a garden tent. By some slight error the numbers on a Victorian solid silver milk jug and a non-vintage plated cream jug had been transposed. The steward held up the items in the wrong order, the audience bid according to the description in the catalogue, and before you could say 'Jack Robinson' there was a nice muddle to be sorted out, as well as a few red faces on and around the platform!

The list of sale goods in front of the auctioneer and the two clerks should have columns for the lot number, the description, the reserve price, and any bid received in advance of the sale, plus blank columns for the price bid and the name of the bidder. If the lists are in sheets of 20 items, the clerk can hand the completed ones to clerk number 2, who can be ready to marry up the details of the lots sold with the various buyers and stand by to take the money.

If all your helpers are new to the joys of running a sale, it is not going too far to have a small rehearsal, with the volunteer auctioneer calling out fictitious lot numbers, names and knocked-down prices and the bookkeepers entering up the details.

The fun starts when several purchasers cannot remember the lots they bought, or how much they bid for them, the auctioneer knocked two lots down to 'Roberts' when one should have been 'Robins', and lot 44 – described as a lampshade – turns out to be a lampbase. It takes humour and patience, when everybody is tired, to cope with the dénouement and send all the buyers away happily with their purchases and a receipt as proof of payment. Armed with this, they will then be able to get themselves and their purchases past the 'heavies' on the door.

Now all you need – while the volunteer helpers clear the room, stack the chairs and sweep the floor – is peace and quiet for a couple of hours while you work out the discounts. When that is all finalized, you can pay the donors, draw up the accounts and close the books on a successful venture.

Arrangements for a combined meal and sale are obviously somewhat more complicated. For this, it is probably best to split your committee in two, one section to take responsibility for the food and drink and applying for the Occasional Permissions or Justices' 'off' licence (see page 103 for full details) while the other group copes with all the details of the sale itself. A joint committee meeting from time to time will be essential, however, so that the left hand knows exactly what the right is doing.

By careful wording of the invitation you can make the occasion sound very special, and so attract people who might not come to 'just an auction'.

Let's look at some scenarios. For example, how much am I bid for a ticket for a champagne-and-smoked-salmon lunch (that is, wholewheat sandwiches and sparkling wine, plenty of it) in a marquee on the lawn? The goods for sale, on this Saturday in June, range from Victorian whatnots and brass coal-buckets to faded watercolours, some of them of no fixed parentage, and musty books. They are set out in another tent and presided over by an auctioneer having a self-imposed busman's holiday.

Most of the guests have come because the church needs new windows and because the sale is being held at *the* house in the neighbourhood, to which they do not receive too many luncheon invitations. Besides, it is fun to sit and eat at tables of four or six, calling up an occasional bottle of wine and browsing over the catalogue. There is always someone in the party who is a self-acknowledged expert on whatever is on offer, so even before the sale starts the competition will hot up.

After one such sale, which made a total profit of some £6,000, the auctioneer revealed that there were only six 'hard' buyers in the audience, people who consistently went to the limit for the items they wanted. All the others helped – how they helped! – to push the prices up, and were content to go home with one or two token items. Without the champagne buffet and the personal invitation to the big house, there would have been nothing like the profit.

Who'll start me off for a ticket to a wine buffs' supper party and auction in a timbered barn? The guests are served roast beef and jacket potatoes at long trestle tables around the outside – medieval-style – and when it comes to coffee-and-liqueurs time, the auction gets under way on a platform in the centre. This time there is wine for sale, from single bottles of port, encrusted in dust and fetching awe-inspiring prices, all the way down the scale to cases of pink plonk. The auctioneer, in his jolly repartee, knows only too well how to play to the vanity of connoisseurs in the audience, and a sale like this – if you can maximize on both the donations and the audience – is a highly effective way of raising funds. It is also far more fun than buying one's Christmas booze from the supermarket.

Often a member of a local wine firm will come along, for a complimentary ticket to the dinner or supper, and give a short 'spiel' about the wines in the more important lots. This certainly helps to bump up the prices and makes it possible for the auctioneer to concentrate solely on getting the best bids. It is always possible, too, that a friendly wine merchant will be prepared to donate a few 'odd bins' or bottles to the auction on some kind of percentage basis.

With a captive audience of people dining you simply cannot afford *not* to have a raffle going round during the meal. A well-chosen hamper of goodies, including table wine, champagne or port, is a sure way of getting at least an additional £1 a head off the guests, only a few of whom will actually be buying the wines to be auctioned later.

If you have wine to sell by auction, and you will be selling it in lots of less than 9 litres, or one case of 'standard' 75-cl bottles (in which event it counts as wholesaling, and is exempt), you will need a licence. If of course you are combining a lunch or supper party with the sale, you will apply for a licence anyway. Auctioneers will tell you not to bother with this – and many of them do not – but that is how the law stands.

What's the bidding for an admission ticket to a mulled-wine-and-mince-pie party followed by a Christmas sale? The venue is no problem (the school hall) and the time is about right, mid-November. The children have been pestering the life out of aunts, uncles and grannies for months to make toys, gifts and decorations, or to make up mini-hampers of preserves, groceries and fruit. The senior children do all the fetching and carrying, make the lists, set out the tables, polish the glasses and so forth. They do not actually bid for the goods – excitement could then run *too* high – but they have ways of instructing their parents accordingly.

The drinks are easy. Cheap red wine takes on a new importance when it is heated gently with cloves, cinnamon, nutmeg, orange and lemon juice, and the junior version, using red grape juice, is just as delicious. In olden days wine was put in pans and heated with a red hot poker. There is no need to go to those lengths, however: electric crockpots are the ideal solution to 'outside catering'. If several people on the committee bring cooking pot and plug (both clearly marked with their names to avoid later confusion) and plug them into the school kitchen, the wine can be left to simmer gently and, with the pots switched to 'low', will keep hot without spoiling.

Turning the Christmas bazaar into a party pays dividends. Although you have the same kind of merchandise to sell, and the same group of people buying, generally speaking, you will find that once the wine and conversation are flowing, a livelier and more profitable occasion results. And that's what it's all about.

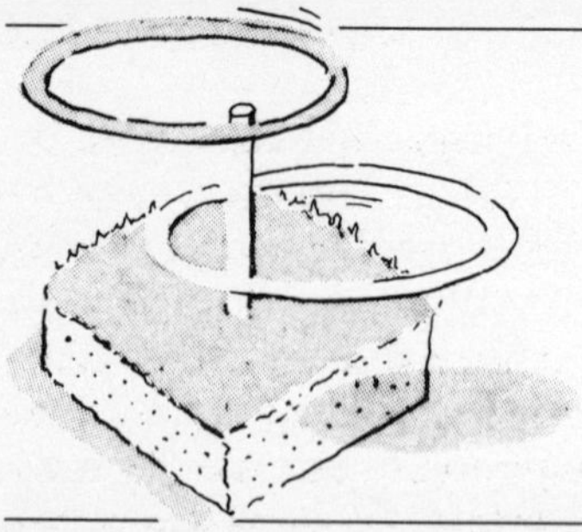

CHAPTER 6

Putting up a good show

Who would have thought it possible before Bob Geldof did it: to put on a show that would raise £50 million and lift fund-raising to new and inspirational heights? Ever since 1985 and Live Aid, the greatest charity show on earth, things will never be the same again. Now there is a new twist to fund-raising and an increased determination to provide the money so desperately needed to get things done. Band Aid, Food Aid, Concert Aid, Dance Aid, School Aid, War Aid, Sports Aid, Fashion Aid, Flower Aid: the very names have an insistent urgency about them.

Raising money for charity has never been more vital. And for those who are neither prepared nor able themselves to undertake a sponsored water-ski jump, organize a supper party or run a stall at a fête, giving money has never been easier.

Now that radio and television stations broadcast day- and night-long appeals, all you have to do, as one presenter put it, is 'Sit down, tune in, phone in or write in, and pay up'. Many of the video clips shown of people bravely trying to overcome hardship or handicap make compelling viewing, too. They also make us aware of the much-needed facilities already provided by the results of earlier appeals, and of the amazing variety of goods generously donated, often by celebrities, for auction.

These programmes have highlighted some remarkable examples of determination, like that of young Oliver, awaiting his second kidney transplant, who raised £1,400 by undertaking a tiring five-mile bicycle ride. His courage, shown on the BBC's *Children in Need* appeal, encouraged one viewer to phone in with an offer to purchase two kidney dialysis machines. We have also been shown wonderful facilities like the toy libraries, set up by a couple who are themselves handicapped, where disabled children can play with a whole range of exciting (and, incidentally, expensive) specialized toys for several hours a day. They can even take them home, which many joyfully do.

Among the lots we have seen going under the fund-raising hammer have been a huge fruitcake baked and decorated by a scout group and a hand-made Tudor-style doll's house complete in every detail; these are just two items among dozens and dozens more, all going for a good cause to the highest telephone bidder. All this heartwarming effort and generosity, coupled with persistent appeals from the presenters and guest celebrities, make it practically impossible to sit comfortably at home and not feel obliged to pick up the phone, get out a credit card or write a pledge letter. And that, of course, is the whole idea.

From the dizzy heights which broadcast appeals can reach, we come down to earthly levels. Putting on a show for charity at a local level can be one of the most rewarding ways to raise funds, involving as it does a group of people working together for a common goal. One of the most poignant examples of this, a case of Band Aid close to home, was a concert held in memory of one of our neighbours, a 12-year-old boy named Richard, who died from brittle bone disease. Incredibly, he had written a will, leaving everything he had in his piggy bank and savings account to his own pet charity, Guide Dogs for the Blind.

That was inspiration enough, with his parents giving the lead, for a series of events to be held spontaneously 'for Richard's dogs'. The main one was a concert organized by teachers at his school, doing what they normally do – teach music. Members of the school band practised a programme of predominantly woodwind pieces in their spare time for six weeks until, as near perfect as could be, they were ready to stage a concert in a church hall. Printing for the posters and programmes was donated or carried out at cost, parents of children at the school provided refreshments, and the event was a sell-out. At the end of the evening the youngsters gave vent to their feelings by singing 'Morning has broken' and 'Amazing Grace'. As a result the goal, to train and adopt a guide dog to be called Richard, came £206 closer. A disco for 5- to 12-year-olds brought in another £80, a toy and tuck sale in a garden, organized by a couple of young friends, raised £46, a sponsored walk crossed the finishing post with £150. Richard's favourite cause is over £1,100 the richer for his memory now, and a photograph of the trained guide dog which carries his name has pride of place in his parents' home.

Sometimes a desire to raise money can be the means of finding a solution to a serious social problem, or at least provide a short-term answer. For as long as I can remember, the question of whether or not school pupils should be required to wear uniform or not has exercised the minds of parents, pupils and teachers alike. And ne'er the three shall agree! However, the matter has at last been settled amicably and charitably at one enterprising co-educational high school, with an idea which others would perhaps find it no hardship to follow. Pupils shed their uniform for a day and dressed instead as Swiss milk-maids, American footballers, babies in prams – whatever took their fancy. Teachers, not to be left out in the sartorial cold, dressed as pupils, with more than a hint of St Trinian's about them. For this privilege, in a fun venture which was at once dubbed School Aid, they had to pay heavily, in cash or kind. In cash they raised £200 for cystic fibrosis and in kind they filled 18 sacks with dry stores for Ethiopian famine relief. As to how much school work was achieved that day, I have to report that there was a total news black-out on the subject.

Since that other event that attracted a complete news embargo, the Reagan-Gorbachev Geneva Summit, it seems almost invidious to mention that 16 members of the Essex Wargaming Society staged an imaginary Third World War; but for once hostilities were all in a good cause. This 48-hour table-top version of fierce conflict between NATO and Warsaw Pact countries was settled – as perhaps all disagreements should be – on a mixture of tactics and the roll of dice, and two referees ensured that there was no foul play amongst the 1,000 lead soldiers. The outcome of this good-natured War Aid was £400 for Action Research for Multiple Sclerosis.

Every locality has a wealth of talent in the clubs,

societies, groups, shops, businesses and individuals that make up its community. Scan your area for a friendly neighbourhood team or expert who could get together with your own organization and help you to raise money. Fashion shows, wine-tastings, hairdressing, beauty and flower-arranging demonstrations, they all have consumer interest and cash potential.

Fashion Aid is a phrase that trips lightly off the tongue now, a new phrase to describe a fund-raising event that has been popular for a long time. Proprietors of fashion shops, sports outfitters and boutiques are usually pleased to put on a display of their latest ranges, the local equivalent of the London or Paris collections. They provide the clothes and models, you provide the venue, the catwalk and enough refreshments to make it feel like a party – and well worth the entrance fee. Ask someone with a lively personality and a good microphone manner – perhaps a disc jockey or presenter from the local radio station – to do the honours ('This is Sharon wearing the very latest in leisure wear for a spring holiday in Outer Mongolia' and so on) and you could be on to a winner.

Unlike fashion models, fashion shows come in all shapes and sizes. If you are co-operating with the swishest shop in town, make it a ritzy affair and serve dainty asparagus rolls, smoked salmon sandwiches, tiny teacakes and champagne. If the models will be cartwheeling through the programme in tracksuits and trainers, back up the healthy, sporting image with crunchy crudités, wholewheat flans and pizza, wine, apple juice and spa water. Or for a trendy boutique evening, serve bubbly mixer drinks and snappy canapés. At one such event held recently, a hairdressing student offered to give members of the audience – who might otherwise have felt out of things – 'instant punk', using on-the-spot washable sprays of whatever combination of colours you care to mention (pink, green and silver topped the poll) for £1 a time. There was scarcely a brown or grey head in the hall by the end of the evening. And it must have meant good business for the hairdresser next day. Perhaps he would like to stage his own hairdressing demo, another time . . .?

A wine-tasting evening can be a great attraction, and

most local wine merchants will enter into the spirit of the thing magnificently and profitably. The system is that, for a nominal charge, they bring the glasses and a selection of wines from any part of the world and in any price range you deem suitable. A member of their staff leads the audience gently up and down the northern and southern slopes of the vineyards under review – without actually going to the lengths of telling them that they will be amused by the presumptiousness of these delightful little wines. And with each new vineyard comes another tray with tiny glasses of the wine to be tasted. The sultry scenery, the colour and condition of the grape, the whole fascinating process of wine-making comes to life and, as the wines keep coming, your guests feel thoroughly spoiled. You supply tiny cubes of cheese and dry biscuits for the serious business of the evening, and after that it is up to you. If you wish provide a light buffet supper, then you can charge more for the tickets and there will be more profit in the occasion. Organize a raffle or two – vital for the funds, when everyone is on such a 'high' – and there will be more still.

It is not every day you see a queue a quarter of a mile long in the high street nowadays, so that must mean that antiques road shows are a good thing. The queue in question had formed two-and-a-half hours before the doors were due to open on a fund-raising event generously hosted in the town hall by a local dealer. He came armed with a selection of good talking-point items from his shop and a couple of specialists from his staff who could bring the world of pottery, glass, furniture and paintings vividly to life. Customers were invited along either just to listen to the spiel or to bring their own treasures for identification and valuation. It is always fascinating to be told that Granny's old sugar bowl is probably the only one of its kind still in existence, or that the book you use to hold up a desk lid is a first edition and really should be treated with more respect. So fund-raisers please note: anything – within reason – that the television companies can do on the screens, and with which they capture people's imaginations, you can cash in on locally. Sell glasses of wine and snacks or, in keeping with the mood of the occasion, madeira and cake, and charge £1 or so admission plus £2 for each consultation; if my past experience is anything to go on, it will be all you can do to encourage the local hopefuls, clutching newspaper parcels and plastic bags, to form an orderly queue and wait their turn.

Pay-as-you-learn could well be the motto for a whole host of fund-raising sessions. You have only to see how fully booked out local day and evening classes become to realize that deep within most of us there must be an eternal thirst for knowledge, even if it is only how to make a better job of icing the Christmas cake or produce an attractive-looking birthday bouquet. Look at your neighbours and friends in a new light to see whether any of them has demonstrator potential. Perhaps there is someone who used to teach classes, who has recently done some interesting research for a book, or who has nimble fingers and a cheery line of patter. For demonstrations of all kinds are a form of entertainment – and perhaps this is where they differ from adult education courses. Who can you come up with? It might be someone who has mastered the art of Chinese cookery and would be willing to reveal the wonders of the wok; someone with an artistic flair who would guide people through the intricacies of cake-decorating; a gifted photographer who would provide some insights into the lure of the lens, or someone who has a special way with flowers. No matter if the individual feels her – or his – forte is doing rather than talking. While she builds up a pedestal arrangement or fashions neat little posies she can tell her audience about her great-grandmother who was head cook to the last tsar, or of the time she rowed single-handed down the Amazon – anything goes, it seems, and it by no means has to relate to the job in hand.

Invite your guests to a private house – if you can find one with a kitchen or sitting room large enough – or a hall where people can sit comfortably and feel at home. Charge an admission fee to include appropriate refreshments and, once you have your audience captivated, surprise them with a raffle or competition.

Flower festivals, long established as a delightful way of raising funds for the Church, are now blossoming in houses, gardens, schools and public buildings. One of the most glorious celebrations of flowers I have seen was staged at Longleat House, the magnificent sixteenth-century Wiltshire home of the Marquess of Bath, by groups from the National Association of Flower Arranging Societies in association with the British Epilepsy Association. For this magnificent six-day Flower Aid, leafy pedestals stood like suits of armour on the oak staircase; flowers filled the flowing bowls on the dining-room table; blooms billowed out beside the books in the library; clinical-looking clusters nestled in the baths and marvellous miniature designs and dainty posies decorated dressing-tables and tea-trays. People love to wander round other people's houses, even if they may not be worthy of the 'stately' designation, so if you have a local group of floral art enthusiasts and an interesting house or hall on offer, this could be one of the gentlest and prettiest ways to fill the coffers.

In almost violent contrast to this, Chelmsford prison was the scene of the first dash for freedom when members of the Round Table dressed as convicts and staged a pretend break-out. They were sponsored for so much money per county penetrated, and so their object was to enter the highest number of counties in Britain in the shortest possible time, all suitably attired in pyjama-style 'convict' gear, of course. The winning team of four 'lags', leaving the Essex gaol on a Saturday morning, clocked up 806 miles and 36 counties in a breathtaking 15 hours' drive.

They need not have bothered. There is a chap who lives not all that many miles from there who makes a run for it with nothing like so much hassle. Escapologist Simon Lovell's ploy is to get himself into a straitjacket, have someone tie him up and then haul him up to the very top of a building-site crane. 'Get yourself out of that one,' people are inclined to say as he disappears above cloud level.

And he does: frequently . . . for charities.

CHAPTER 7

Leading them a merry dance

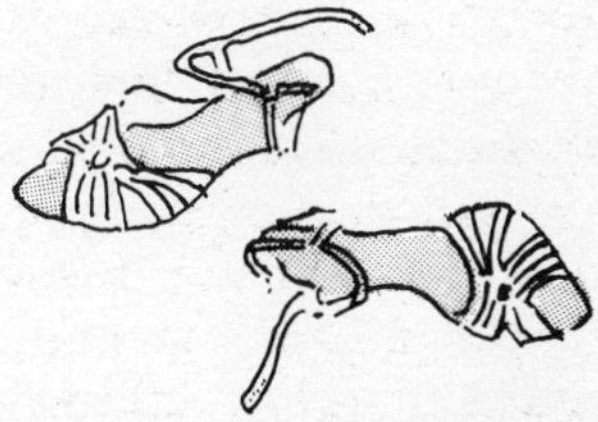

Almost every large fund-raising campaign has one. They are more popular at some times of year than others. Different age groups have widely differing views on what type is 'normal'. You can have them indoors or out. Some halls are specially licensed to hold them. There can be quite a bit of profit in them, but they are hard work. I refer, of course, to dances.

Some fund-raising committees hold one as a getting-to-know-each-other social event, bringing together people who will be working side by side in the future to raise a formidable amount of cash. Sometimes a dance is the icing on the cake, held as a final flourish, a thank-you, a 'haven't-we-done-well?' occasion when the target figure is almost topped. And sometimes a dance is just for the fun of it, and the funds.

First come the decisions. Decide what age group you will be targeting and then plan the dance accordingly. Soft lights and sweet music, strains of the valeta and memories of yesteryear; flashing lights and sounds that will throb in the ears for days to come; or one of the many possibilities in between: dances are highly individual affairs and it is almost impossible to please all the people all of the time.

Pool your experiences of bands, groups and discos that have performed at other functions. If someone recommends a group, but no one can remember where and when they played, find out whether they have an engagement locally in the near future and try to arrange for someone to look in, however briefly, to judge the mood of the occasion. The band sets the tempo of the evening in more ways than one, and it is essential to make the right choice. The date of your function might well rest on the availability of the group. Popular performers are often booked solid for a year ahead, so book early to avoid disappointment. When you book, tell the manager or leader the type of function you are planning, whether there is a special theme (Valentine's Day, St Patrick's Day or whatever), the approximate numbers and age range of the guests, how long you plan for the supper interval, whether you will have any back-up music or cabaret at that time, and whether you would like one of their number to act as master of ceremonies for the evening.

Put all this in writing when you send a deposit and, if your venue is at all out of the way, enclose a map. Even that is not foolproof. We once booked a West Indian steel band from Ipswich to play in a barn in Great Bardfield, in Essex, and sent a map clearly marked with a 'we are here' red arrow. We wrote a week before the event to re-confirm all the arrangements, got the barn ready and, figuratively speaking, sat back and waited. Seven o'clock came. The band did not. We rang the leader's home and his wife assured us that they had left in plenty of time. Seven-thirty. Still no band. Eight o'clock and the first guests started to arrive. We went home, had a stiff drink, returned with some tapes and played them – loudly. Nine o'clock, and the band tumbled out of their mini-bus, hot-foot from Great Barford, in Bedfordshire. Man, had they had a terrible time trying to find a town hall near a T-junction with a massive timbered barn next to it . . . In the event, all was well that ended well: the band played on, and on, deep into the night. And as a 'sorry-we-messed-you-about' gesture they composed a calypso there and then, and sang it to 'Lady Pameela'. Even without that, there would have been no hard feelings. They are a super crowd, and could find that village blindfold by now. They have been back every year for ten years and there is nearly always a waiting list for tickets.

Assess your collective capabilities for running a dance with no outside help, which is one of the surest ways to maximize on the profit potential, and also take stock of suitable venues in your area. For a ball on a grand scale, you could opt for an hotel or country club, where the catering and all services would be provided, or, if you are lucky enough to have the use of one for the asking, a spacious house where you could do the catering. In the summer, you could hold a ball in a marquee, and there again you could employ professional caterers or not, as you wish. Village halls, town halls, scout and guide halls, sports clubs and pavilions all have, to a varying degree, the facilities you will need, though some of them may lack the style. Farm buildings, storage sheds and other commercial premises could provide the space, as long as you can provide the ingenuity to decorate them to create a happy and relaxed atmosphere.

The size of the venue is important. There is nothing more chilly than a hundred or so people trying to look like a happy crowd in a massive outhouse. Far better to screen off just the section you need and decorate it until it does look suitably small and intimate. For tips on transforming unpromising venues, see the chapter entitled 'Temporary Accommodation'.

Whether the dance is held in a barn or a backyard, a hall or a hotel will affect more than just the style of the occasion. Many public halls, clubrooms and hotel ballrooms are licensed for music and dancing. Most barns, private houses, aircraft hangars, warehouses and business premises are not. If you are organizing a performance of live music in unlicensed premises or in the open air and the proceeds are going to a cause that is not a registered charity, you should write to the Performing Right Society (address on page 160) to ask for a permit for a one-off event, explaining what organization or fund will be receiving the profits. The Society will consider whether or not to waive the royalty fee. It is not the end of the world if it does not. At the time of writing the minimum 'one-off' fee is about £7.00, though it varies according to the seating capacity of the premises.

It is much the same when you hire a disco, or play any type of recorded music. Here it is Phonographic Performance Ltd which takes an interest. Write, giving similar information, to the address on page 160, and the company will give you its verdict. Registered charities need not apply: they are usually exempt from paying such royalties under the provisions of the Copyright Act, 1956.

It is an offence to play live or recorded music to members of a club or to the public without either exemption or permission, because many composers, lyricists and recorded performers rely on such royalties for a living; it is also a trap for the unwary, and probably one that a great many organizers fall into quite unwittingly.

In describing various ways of raising funds I come back again and again to giving the event a theme, as a way of capturing the public's imagination: not 'Come to our dance in the scouts' hut' but 'Come to our Roaring Twenties Dance'. It is a bit like the difference between saying 'This is my sister', and 'This is my sister, Anne-Marie.' Now she is someone, with her own individuality and personality.

Sometimes the season will suggest an ever-popular theme – Midsummer, Hallowe'en, New Year's Eve and so on. Sometimes one of the committee will have a flash of inspiration, start describing how the hall could be decorated, what food could be served to follow through the theme, and so on. If this carries the committee members away on a wave of enthusiasm, that is just how it should be. Once the committee is wholeheartedly behind an idea, the tickets are half-way to being sold.

What is it to be? Why not take your partners for a Roaring Twenties Dance? Some of the girls have entered into the spirit of it by sticking beads and braid around the hems of mini-dresses and sporting headbands. Some of the men have come in blazers and flannels, and the first 'free' drink is a choice of a pink or green (not-too-alcoholic) cocktail, complete with red and green cherries on sticks.

Pink, green and red are the colour theme for the evening. Pinned in loops across the front of the buffet tablecloth is a swag of soft evergreenery and paper carnations. There are pink wipe-clean paper cloths on all the supper tables, and small green and pink flower-arrangements made in plastic saucers, the containers concealed by their contents. Huge bunches of paper flowers decorate the stage and a bowl of them, mixed with trailing ivy, stands on a pedestal by the entrance.

The buffet supper is simple but delicious, with cold chicken breast in a pink mayonnaise and pimento sauce, green salad and tomato salad. The puddings are light and fluffy, like the mood of the occasion: there is a choice of strawberry mousse or gooseberry fool, with pink sponge-finger biscuits.

Two couples from a local theatrical group, dressed to

dazzle, have come to demonstrate the charleston, the black bottom and the one-step; afterwards, everyone joins in, has an on-the-spot lesson, and then away they go, dancing and bubbling like champagne.

The raffle girls – also dressed to dazzle – have cinema-usherette boxes on straps, pink and green raffle tickets (of course), and are gently but surely extracting money for the chance to win a tableful of prizes: bottles of gin, aperitifs, perfume, cosmetics and fun jewellery.

They are not the only prizes of the evening. Continuing the theme of the times there are spot prizes too, heralded by delighted ooohs and aahs as the music stops and the light swivels to search out each lucky couple. (If prizes are not donated, do not forget to include their cost in the price of the tickets.)

Another possibility, moving from the sublime to the gor blimey, is a Tramps' Supper: come as you are, complete with old clothes, dirty faces and, ideally, two days' growth (women are excused the latter).

Paper and card scarecrows and cartwheels make strong silhouettes around the walls, and there is a mock camp-fire on the stage (three crisscrossed sticks and a billy-can suspended over glowing red crêpe-paper embers). Had the fire regulations not positively prohibited them, there would have been bales of straw and sheaves of corn, too.

The supper is served on waxed paper plates (easier to come by than tin), and the food is of course bangers, mash and beans, with chunks of apple pie to follow.

The raffle sellers, as fetching a pair of tramps in baggy suits and flat caps as you could ever hope to see, go round with billy-cans on string begging a coin or two, mister, for the kind of prizes tramps and others know how to appreciate – whisky, gin and a box of groceries. Some wit has conned a voucher out of the local dry cleaner's, too.

No one, but no one, can stop their feet tapping to the infectious rhythm of a West Indian steel band. We used to send out invitations to a wide circle of people in the village reckoning that some were much more likely to come than others. You could never be certain either way. One old lady, in her ninety-first year, rang up and said our invitation had been sitting on her mantelpiece, calling to her, and at last she had made up her mind to come. 'We four girls were never allowed to go to dances, so I've never been in the habit of it,' she explained. 'But I thought this time I will go.'

And come she did, sitting just inside the door – not too near the band – tapping her stick to the beat and receiving callers. When we drove her home at the end of the evening – she would not dream of going earlier – she proudly told us that 26 people had come up to speak to her, and seven had asked her to dance. There then followed a lesson in how politely to refuse an invitation when the sands of time have rather caught up with you.

Barns and large halls are ideal for a Caribbean dance. You can usually get posters of palm trees and golden beaches from a local travel agent or the West Indian tourist board. Boughs of greenery representing those tantalizing palms and, if the hall needs cheering up, wide bands of crêpe paper around the walls at blue-sky level, will set the scene. The band usually does its best to leave nothing more to the imagination.

A supper of honey-roast ham, rice and pineapple salad and black-bean salad, with treacle tart and coconut meringues to follow, is about as near to Caribbean cuisine as many guests will want to get: easy to prepare, and delicious too.

Of all the bands I know, our friends from the West Indies seem most anxious to play special request numbers. Ask members and friends to note them down before the dance starts. If the band plays someone's special favourite at the beginning of the evening, how can he or she resist jumping up to dance, and bringing the rest of the table with them?

Evil witches, black cats and a cauldron of something nasty might not sound like the perfect recipe for a convivial evening, but Hallowe'en dances do seem to draw the crowds. Unless you have some artistic types among the group, budget for a little expenditure on sleek-eyed cat masks, ghoulish garlands, life-like (or death-like) skeleton cut-outs, swooping bats and owls; and order a packet or two of 'eerie' poppers, which shoot out ghastly streamers, for good measure. There is an amazing range of Hallowe'en nasties in a 'novelties' catalogue (address on page 160) which is pretty well guaranteed to get every dance off to a terrifying start.

Considering the time of year, and the fact that it could be a chilly night, mulled wine with slices of apple bobbing a-top the spiced and steaming brew would make the ideal drink. Frankfurters and kebabs in long rolls, with lots of pickles and chutneys, jacket potatoes and salad take care of the first course. For dessert there could be chocolate cup-cakes with piped-on be-whiskered faces, toffee apples on sticks and generous slices of pumpkin pie. The pies, of course, are made with the flesh scooped out of the pumpkins used for candle decorations.

You do not need all that much of the blarney to sell tickets for a St Patrick's Day dance in the middle of March, nor do you need to consult an Irish soothsayer to find out how to decorate the hall. Go for green and shamrocks all the way. Get people in the mood by bringing in a couple of Irish pipers, or asking a local folk-dance club if they could put on a demonstration of the Irish jig. After a couple of whiskies most of the guests will feel confident enough to join in.

A light casserole of lamb would be a tasty choice for the supper – stew is not the best of things to dance on. Call it something like 'Galway hotpot' and serve it with jacket potatoes with lots of butter and chopped herbs. Blarney trifle, pepped up with a dash of whiskey from the Emerald Isle, would round off the supper nicely.

Make a little extra cash and cause a bit of fun by having a side-show of a huge blarney stone to kiss. People will be queuing up to part with their money if you assure them that wishes are always – well, sometimes – granted. And while they are in the mood, there could be a curtained-off area where Mother Macree will read their palms – as long as they cross hers with silver. The raffle prizes virtually choose themselves: Irish whiskey, liqueur and linen and, if your local garden centre has one, a pot of real shamrock.

You have to know your clientele quite well before you decide to hold a square dance. It is not everyone's cup of tea, and tickets for such an event can meet with quite a bit of sales resistance. But if you have a crowd who are not afraid to stand up and be counted – there is quite a bit of that to be done – and sometimes make fools of themselves, then it can be tremendous fun.

Actually, a square dance is one of the easiest events to organize because the caller (who comes with the special square-dance band) and the guests do all the work. A team starts things off by demonstrating the first dance, always a simple one, then everyone has to join in. A good caller will not countenance anyone sitting out for a second – that can be part of the trouble. The dances get progressively harder but if all goes well people get progressively more confident, and soon everyone is swinging their partners – and enjoying it.

Food can be as informal as the occasion – sausages in rolls, cheese rolls and other finger foods, or something like cold beef and salads. That is about all the caller will allow time for!

On the other side of the coin, there are those functions where the meal is the main attraction and the dancing becomes incidental. In the summer one of our local village-hall committees decided to branch out from its usual annual fund-raising disco by having a pig-roast on the playing-field. There was a marquee for the supper tables and the hall was used, as usual, for dancing. It was a sell-out, and the committee's biggest problem now is working out how it can expand the event next year to accommodate the stampede.

Discos organize themselves. The people who run them have everything so incredibly well planned – at least, I have never yet come across one that was not – that virtually all you need to provide is an electrical socket. They bring everything it takes to create that amazing sound, the flashing lights and the patter that keeps the excitement at fever-pitch the whole evening long. This leaves the committee blissfully free to concentrate on other things, such as the pig-roast.

In this case, almost as soon as the ink was dry on the minutes of the committee meeting, one of the members saw that there was another roast taking place a few miles away. He got on his bike, watched two porkers gently rotating on stout and efficient home-made spits and asked to borrow them. After all, it was all in – another – good cause. Back at the ranch, no one felt quite man enough for the job of carving twice 100–110 pounds weight of sizzling pork, which is about what it takes to feed, very generously, 150 people. So the pigs were not ordered from a local farmer – the obvious option in our part of the world – but from the butcher. His services on the night then came free.

For weeks before the event bands of voluntary Good King Wenceslases went out gathering sticks and stumps for the fire – you need quite a pile to keep the embers glowing from eight in the morning until the party starts at eight in the evening. The crackling does not crackle if the ardour of the fire cools, so that is a job-and-a-half in itself.

A dark green and serviceable marquee was borrowed from the scouts (it is always worth asking local groups if they have one) and kitted out with folding tables and chairs round the sides. The bar, at one end, was dispensing beer, cider, wine and soft drinks about as fast as the helpers could go. Down the centre of the marquee stretched the buffet-tables, laden with all kinds of salads, pickles, relishes, mustards, hot garlic and herb breads, butter pats and, for dessert, Black Forest gâteaux.

Then, through the tent flaps marched the butcher and his mate, holding aloft first one pig and then another. It was quite a night – so much so that many of the guests clean forgot to get up and dance. The disco organizer for once had the hardest job of all.

Whenever you are relying on a dance to make a really large profit, say in the region of £1,000 or more, try sending Cinderella to a Grand Ball at the most prestigious local venue – a large house, an hotel or a swish marquee on a lawn. On such an occasion you can really go to town. Have programmes printed that include a foreword by a well-known local personality in support of the charity or cause, the supper menu, a list of the speakers or those who will propose the toasts, and another list of the people and firms who have donated prizes. All that provides a vehicle for selling advertisements to those same local businesses, and a splendid way of making a clear profit. Sometimes, depending of course on how many guests you have and how much, therefore, you are able to charge for the advertisements, the programme alone can make well over £250.

At this kind of event, where the tickets may well cost £15 or more each, people do not expect to come for a cheap night out. A tombola is a must – the biggest money-spinner of all. Guests will keep slipping out of their seats, drawn to it like magnets, and the tables will soon fill up with an assortment of prizes. This is just the time for the raffle-ticket sellers to come round. Once people get the idea they are on a winning streak, there is no holding them!

Whatever the theme you choose for your dance, if the tickets can be designed with a small line drawing depicting it – a mask, a glass of fizzing champagne, a Valentine heart or whatever – that, too, will capture the eye of the beholder and assist sales.

Most printers will number the tickets for you. If they do not, then you must, so that you have a complete record of who has sold which ticket to whom. Then, on the evening, have someone on the door taking tickets, tearing them in half and giving back the unnumbered half for the guest to hand over for any first 'free' drink, or for their buffet supper. After all, if you are entertaining a large crowd of people you do not know, it would be the easiest thing in the world for those with hearty appetites to go round again and again piling up their plates and completely throwing out the careful calculations of the caterers. But if they have handed in a ticket half, this problem cannot arise. If there is food to spare once everyone has been served, and 'seconds' are announced, then that is another matter.

Whether or not to handle the catering yourselves is perhaps one of the toughest decisions to take, and one which depends entirely on how many willing and capable pairs of hands are at your disposal. It may be that you can compromise by asking a local professional caterer to cook the main course and your own helpers to provide a galaxy of puddings. Perhaps the chapter entitled 'Feeding the Multitude' (pages 96-117) will help you to assess what, if you decide on self-catering, you are letting yourselves in for.

If you do decide to employ a caterer, this will obviously affect your costs, and therefore your ticket price, significantly. It is a decision that needs to be taken early on. The caterer will offer you a choice of menus at a range of prices on a per head basis. Check that this price includes the hire of any crockery, cutlery and serving dishes (though many public halls have their own adequate stocks) and that there will be no extras (delivery, for instance).

Calculate your other expenses: the hall, band, any serving and washing-up staff, ticket and poster printing and so on. Estimate the profit you would hope to make from the raffle and any other games of chance. And then do your sums. Is a profit of, say, £1 each on one hundred tickets worth all the effort? Could the ticket price stand an increase over the figure you first thought of? Should you run another attraction – a tombola or a raffle, for example – to boost the profits? Fund-raising is all about making the maximum possible profit in ratio to the work involved.

Liquid refreshments are of course essential at any dance. That means that whoever is going to run the bar, a licence will be needed. If you ask a local publican to do it, give him at least six weeks' notice and he will get the necessary permission. If you are going to handle it yourselves, think more than once. To run a 'full bar' with all that entails – a range of spirits, aperitifs, beers, mixers and wines – can turn out to be disappointing from the profit point of view: think of all those half-used bottles at the end of the evening. And a bar does need several reasonably experienced staff to cope with the rush periods – when people first arrive, just before and after supper, and when the MC announces that the bar is about to close. It is certainly possible to do it, as long as you have adequate and reliable help. If you order the drink through a brewery, it can apply for the Justices' 'off' licence for you. Or you can apply for an 'Occasional Permission' licence for your organization (for more details see page 103).

It is best to be quite clear in advance about who, if anyone, is going to buy drinks for the members of the band, for whom a whole evening's playing will be thirsty – and expensive – work. Sometimes a member of the committee will take this on as his contribution. Sometimes the committee will agree to buy one drink out of the funds and expect the band to finance themselves for the rest. It is as well for the committee to decide before the event and then stick to what was agreed.

If you can, check up in advance whether any of the guests is likely to be out on a limb during the evening. A charity dance is just the kind of function people will attend because they believe in the cause and want to play their part. Go through the list to see which guests might not know many others, and have someone on hand to introduce them to committee members and friends. It goes without saying that we all do this at our own private parties. But somehow a public function seems different, and everyone is so busy attending to their own duties, rushing about putting last-minute touches to the tables and food, running the bar and selling raffle tickets, that it is all too easy to forget about the guests as people. Yet we have all known that moment of near-panic, on entering a room full of people who all seem to know each other, when we have wished the floor would open up beneath us. How much better it is if one of the committee, anticipating that this might happen, comes up and says, 'Hello, you're Jean, aren't you? We were wondering whether you'd like to join us at our table.'

The placing of the tables at a supper-dance can be about as fraught with diplomatic wrangles as the seating plan for a summit conference. We had a massive breakdown in committee communication once. One faction decided that the buffet-tables would be set in a long line down the centre of the hall and chairs would be placed – wallflower-fashion, backs to the wall – around three sides of the room. About the only dance you could have performed in the space in between was the conga, and then only if you did not do the side-kicks. No tables for guests to eat on? 'Let them eat on their laps,' someone said firmly as the available card-tables and bright gingham cloths were firmly packed away again.

That group went home to start cooking the rice. Others arrived, threw up their hands in horror and arranged the buffet-tables under the stage, with card-tables and folding chairs filling up the rest of the room. This still left no room for people to circulate before supper, and certainly no room to dance. 'Well, they can push all the tables up together after supper. That'll be soon enough to start dancing,' said someone who was clearly unaware that the band had cost £120.

It was not until the second team of furniture-removers had gone home to heat up their crockpots full of curry that order was restored. The chap who had taken the trouble to draw up a to-scale floor-plan – and then kept its very existence to himself – arrived with his band of henchmen. Apparently it had been the intention all along to serve the food from a small ante-room, from which it could easily and inconspicuously be cleared away, put tables and chairs around the perimeter of the main room and leave the centre free for dancing.

If the music is being provided by a disco and the audience is 'mixed' – some who are switched on to the Big Sound and some who keep asking why on earth they cannot turn it down – it is almost essential not only to serve supper in a separate room but to have seating there too, as a haven for tired ears.

On the subject of noise, if the function is being held in a built-up area, say in a hall in the centre of a residential estate, do spare a thought for the neighbours (who may gladly give you a donation for the cause – and double it if you do not keep them awake half the night). Functions held in a village hall near us have no need of a hired cabaret: they can rely with total confidence on one appearing at 11.30 pm sharp, when the septuagenarian who lives opposite arrives in pyjamas and dressing-gown to bawl out the assembled company for making a noise and threaten the direst of consequences for disturbance of the peace – and of his night's sleep.

When someone is annoyed to this extent, the drill is to telephone the police, who will visit the venue and assess the problem. If they consider the noise level is too high, taking into account the proximity of the neighbours, they will ask for it to be lowered. All this can put something of a damper on proceedings. So, as the evening advances and the noise level soars, consider having a word in the bandleader's ear.

Almost every large fund-raising campaign includes a dance at some point. Some are more enjoyable and successful than others. Some are more profitable than others. Let us hope yours will score on all counts.

CHAPTER 8

Feeding the multitude

Sunday brunch at the rectory, a Mexican beano in the school hall, a curry tiffin in a supporter's home, strawberry tea on the lawn, a soup kitchen in the scouts' hut, a formal dinner in the village hall – there is no end to the number of ways you can invite your guests to eat, drink and be merry, and at the same time help you to raise funds.

Even though you may be dealing with recipes in the 'take three dozen eggs' category, there is nothing at all difficult about catering in quantity. It simply requires meticulous planning at every stage, from the choice of menu and setting of a budget, through the allocation of tasks, to the actual shopping, preparation, cooking, transport and presentation.

The size of the venue and its facilities (the hall, barn, house or whatever), the time of year and the amount of help you can muster will all play a part in determining what kind of meal is practicable. Is the room large enough for people to sit at tables or perch a plate on their laps? Are the kitchen facilities adequate for preparing, or even heating through, a full-scale hot meal? Will any foods be particularly plentiful and well priced – will there, for example, be pick-your-own salads, vegetables or soft fruits available? What can you offer within the given budget? Have you enough willing cooks to provide the broth? And what types of dishes are the cooks most familiar with? This is a key question. It is no good someone coming along with a handful of complicated recipes if the people who will actually be doing the cooking are likely to be reduced to a state of nervous collapse on the night.

Once the cooking sub-committee (affectionately known as the 'catering mob' in our group) gets round the table, it comes down to saying, 'If we have a curry party, who's prepared to make the curry? Can three of you cope with 4½ pounds of meat each? And who's going to be responsible for the rice? Can four of you share it between you?' If you sense the slightest lack of confidence or enthusiasm at this stage, now is the time to opt for a fork-and-finger buffet or a cheese-and-wine party, for which everything can be done in advance and (with luck) there will not be any last-minute panics.

The golden rule is always to work comfortably within your resources. If you are embarking on a long fund-raising campaign and planning the first of many functions, be content to learn, as a committee, to walk before you try to run. Put on a simple meal, even a selection of snacks, so that helpers get used to working together as a team. Then it will be easy to set your sights higher. The selection of menus at the end of this chapter, each with an indication of how much work is involved, should help you keep the enterprise within manageable bounds.

Next, coupled with the choice of menu, comes the shopping. It makes sense to plan all the dishes around food that is seasonal, plentiful and cheap – when it will also be at its best and most delicious. Do you have any 'pick-your-own' farms nearby? Perhaps a couple of helpers could enjoy a pleasant afternoon picking raspberries, strawberries, runner beans, sweetcorn, apples. Think of all the contacts you have on the committee, among supporters and even friends-of-friends. Does anyone have a large garden with surplus crops, a contact with a market gardener who might give a favourable discount or toss in a box of vegetables for the good of the cause, or a poultry farmer who might donate the eggs and sell some chickens at cost? For one reason or another it is often easier for business people and individuals to make their donations in kind rather than in cash. By asking them to help, you give them the chance to do so.

Does anyone in your group have a shopping card for a wholesale warehouse? This would provide a good source of large boxes of butter pats, table napkins by the hundred, large tins of coffee, all the in-bulk items you need. Do not overlook your local street market for trays of apples, pears and peaches, nets of onions, baskets of mushrooms and so forth. With a cheery word the week before the event, a nod's as good as a wink when it is for charity, and the price will come tumbling down. Do not forget your own local shops, either, especially if you regularly deal with a small independent retailer. I make a point of buying at least one main item, such as the bread, locally – it seems only fair – and I do not even have to ask for a discount.

As you account for each main item of planned expenditure a picture of the cost structure will build up. You already know the cost, if any, of hiring the hall, chairs, tables and other equipment. The raffle organizer will have estimated the hoped-for profit on a tombola, raffle or other money-making attraction. Now as you fill in the estimated costs of your food shopping list the final pieces in the expenditure jigsaw will fall into place. This is a crucial stage, and by pulling every string you can, tapping every contact and shopping wisely you can make an enormous contribution, in ratio terms, to the eventual profit.

Estimating the quantity of food you need to feed a crowd can be something of a conundrum. It is easy enough for a fork-and-finger buffet, when all you have to do is multiply the number of guests by the number of sausage rolls and vol-au-vents you think they will eat (four or five, say), and allocate the cooking accordingly. The strange thing is that such simple arithmetic does not work when it comes to serving casseroles, vegetables and salads. You do not take a recipe for four people and multiply it by ten to serve 40. You do not even take a recipe for 20 and multiply it by two. The fact is – and there is no entirely logical explanation for it – that the larger the numbers you are catering for, the lower the proportion of food you need (which, in terms of cost of ingredients, is good news for the treasurer). If, for example, you follow a recipe which in quantities for four people allows 150–200 g/6–7 oz of boneless meat per portion, you can confidently cut this down to 125 g/5 oz each for 20 guests and 100 g/4 oz each for 40 people. (See also pages 108-9.)

It is the same with flavouring ingredients. Herbs and spices can be a vicious trap for the unwary. What you certainly must not do is translate 5 ml/1 teaspoon chilli powder, in a recipe to serve four, into five times that amount to serve 20. No one could eat it! Flavourings have the capacity to make their aromatic and pungent presence felt through much larger quantities of meat, pulses, vegetables, pasta and rice with virtually no reduction in effect. The best way, when multiplying up recipe quantities, especially where hot spices are concerned, is to use the original quantity, taste the dish and then gradually add a little more as necessary.

I learned this lesson the hard way, making chilli beans for a bonfire party. The dish was meant to be hot, but this was hotter than the bonfire. Of course the cook, busy by now cutting up the apple pies, is always the last to know. It was only after I noticed that one after another the guests were following an ingenious lead, wrapping the beans in a piece of lettuce leaf and swallowing the pungent parcel whole, like an oyster, with a glass of lager, that I cottoned on. (There is not a lot you can do at this stage, except ladle out plain yoghurt as first aid and accept the leg-pulling cheerfully.)

Another point about multiplying up recipes: if you are following instructions devised to serve four or six, never attempt more than four times that amount all in one go. It is better by far to make the dish in two batches, then you will be much more likely to stay in touch and in control. Often the size and range of appliances you have at home will govern the quantities you can handle at any one time, in any case. Though some halls for hire have wonderful kitchen facilities, all stainless steel and shining bright, many do not. When you are preparing a sizeable meal it is best to leave it to the cook-helpers to decide for themselves how much to do at home and how much to do on site. Obviously soup, casseroles and the like are cooked at home and brought ready to be kept hot or gently reheated. It would cost you a fortune in hall-hire fees if you had to pay while a casserole of beef was simmering gently in an expensive hired kitchen for 2½ hours. But jacket potatoes, rice and some vegetables can be a matter of choice.

Memories of four of us in the kitchen of a public hall all getting in one another's way as we struggled to boil, strain and then keep hot enough rice for 200 has placed me firmly in the 'cook-at-home-whenever-possible' lobby. Now we share out the rice between us, cook it just before leaving, run hot water through it to be extra-sure to separate the grains, strain it thoroughly and turn it into large baking trays or mixing bowls. Covered with foil and popped in a low oven or stood in a larger pan of hot water bain-marie style, the rice keeps perfectly for at least a couple of hours.

Keeping food hot or re-heating it when the accommodation is limited can be a problem. Whatever did we do before the days of electric crockpots? Even these do not solve the question of transport, however, as I discovered when I had to do an involuntary emergency stop on a muddy country lane. Crockpots may be all very well for keeping soups, casseroles, vegetables, pasta, rice and mulled wine in tip-top condition for ages – they are – but when it comes to transporting them, there is nothing to beat a pressure cooker with a good old-fashioned snap-on lid. Just for the record, it takes roughly three-and-a-half weeks to lose the smell of curry from the boot of a Panda.

Meteorologically speaking, there is likely to be less of a problem keeping cold foods cool. Even so, moulds, mousses, trifles and salads do lose their 'edge' if they are subjected for too long to the steam-heat of a busy kitchen. Size up any refrigerator space that may be offered by the host or available in the hire-kitchen and allocate it sparingly – you might need a high proportion of it to chill white wines. Ask the helpers to bring chilled desserts, milk, cream and butter as late as possible. Green salads can be washed, dried (a salad spinner is a tremendous help for party quantities), placed in polythene bags and chilled at home until the last minute, too. Almost the last job before serving will be to arrange the salad in bowls and toss it in the dressing.

A help-yourself hot or cold buffet is probably one of the most popular forms of fund-raising meal and serves as a good example of procedure. If all you are planning to do is hand round snacks on a plate, skip the next few paragraphs.

Setting out a buffet-table requires a fine balance between artistry and strategy. It has to look appetizing and inviting, and at the same time be intensely practical. Queuing up for food you have paid good money for can be one of the least jolly aspects of attending a function.

Consider artistry first. The best-laid table plans always leave room for some eye-catching features over and above the food – a tall cascade of flowers, the kind of design that can easily be seen across a crowded room, a pair of flower-encircled candlesticks, a sheaf-of-wheat harvest loaf, a trug of fresh vegetables, a basket of shiny-bright polished apples, small baskets of dried or silk flowers – whatever seems appropriate to the mood of the occasion.

Strategy should be your next concern. Table plans must work. Whenever possible, have at least two serving points and a 'marshal' to collect supper-tickets, divide the queue into two and shepherd people along. Place the buffet-tables so that there can be a steady through-flow of traffic, preferably so that guests come in one door and, carrying their laden plates, go out the other. This seems painfully obvious, but we have all been to parties where this small detail has been overlooked. If everyone is trying to shuffle back and forth and do a U-turn in front of the tables, accidents are bound to happen – and it will be quite obvious what must be done another time.

If you have enough helpers, it is best to serve guests with at least the main dish: the moussaka, casserole, curry or whatever. This is not only quicker, it assists with portion control. Then they can help themselves to salads, add relishes and condiments (do not forget to provide enough pepper and salt pots) and pick up bread, butter, napkins and cutlery at the end.

In my experience, it is a mistake to put all your eggs in one basket, so to speak, and have the entire main course, enough for the whole party, on the table at the beginning. If the food is supposed to be served hot, this will maximize the problem of keeping it hot. Moreover, if you put all the food in a number of small bowls it will create chaos. People will dither. Is this coleslaw the same as that, and if not which looks tastier? This will be maddening for those behind! On the other hand, if you put all the food out in huge dishes and bowls, by the time half the company has been served it will all look shop-soiled: not very appetizing for those at the back.

It is far better, I suggest, to set out, say, half the food at the beginning and make someone responsible for replenishing, dashing back and forth to the kitchen every time she hears the ominous sound of a spoon scraping on the bottom of the container.

You can never have enough spoons. I have a standard buffet-party 'take' list which goes like this: serving spoons, salad servers, soup ladles, bread board and knife, cheese boards and knives, chopping boards and knives, trays, peppers, salts, hotplate, crockpot, electric kettle, multiple socket outlet (for all those plugs), baskets for bread, bowls for sugar, chutneys, mustard; jugs for cream, milk, coffee and water; chopped herbs and sprays for garnishing, cling-wrap and foil (in case anyone brings their food uncovered), washing-up liquid, sink brush, cloths and every clean teatowel in the house.

The layout of the hall or reception room will probably dictate whether you can set out the desserts, cheese and, later, coffee on separate tables, or whether the 'main course' table has to be cleared and set out again. In this case, you need a nice, smiling, bossy-boots person to say firmly that there will be a slight intermission, a natural and frantic break, before the next course is ready.

It may be possible to rationalize what is left of the main course (that means scrape the leftovers into two or three bowls at one end of the table) and announce that 'seconds' are available – just to keep the wolves from the door.

In an ideal world, it is best to have a fresh tablecloth, of paper, linen or whatever, so that you can whip off the old and on with the new, in true restaurant-waiter style. If this seems a bit over the top on cost and organization, at least have some matching paper napkins on hand to cover up any spillages or stains discreetly. It is practically impossible for a table to put on its best party-puddings face if it is half-covered in beetroot jelly.

Serving coffee at the end of a meal seems to present more of a problem than the rest of the menu put together, probably because everyone is tired and getting a little fractious by then. Or maybe it is just that by this time those same helpers should be starting to clear trays of used plates or going round with the raffle again, and they forget all about boiling kettles.

But unless there is a tea-urn in the hall – and there often is – boil the kettles someone must. Have cups, saucers, tiny bowls of sugar and jugs of milk set out on trays. Whether you are using coffee granules or ground coffee, make it in jugs.

For the former, measure in advance how much water the jugs hold, add the right number of spoonfuls of coffee, pour on the water, stir, fill up tray after tray of cups and keep going until there is only one person left to serve – you.

For ground coffee, allow 60 ml/4 tablespoons coffee to each 600 ml/1 pint boiling water, stir, cover the jug, leave it in a warm place (on the cooker, perhaps) for 4 minutes, then pour it through a strainer.

If you are intending to serve alcoholic drinks, bear in mind first and foremost that you will need a licence. There is no way round it. It does not matter whether you are including the wine as a free extra in the price of the ticket, or whether you are merely asking for donations rather than making a specific charge for drinks: it makes not a scrap of difference. You need a licence.

However, a recent change in the law has enabled *bona fide* organizations, whether they are registered as a charity or not, to apply to the licensing justices, through the Clerk to the Magistrates' Court, for 'Occasional Permission'. This entitles the organization to sell or offer drink for consumption on or off the premises ('off' would apply to selling liquor at an auction or giving it as a raffle prize) up to four times a year. The premises must be deemed suitable, the profits must not contribute in any way to private profit or gain, and the Justices may attach any conditions they choose – such as limiting the drinking hours. You can apply for this 'permission' whether your organization is going to run the bar itself or ask a publican or brewer to organize it.

The other way of complying with the law is for a licensee or brewer to apply for a licensee's occasional 'on' licence ('on' denoting consumption on the premises), which costs more. You would need this, for example, if you were into your fifth function for the same organization in the same calendar year.

The wheels of officialdom grind fairly slowly, so apply in plenty of time: three weeks would be the absolute minimum. Give details of the venue, the expected number of guests or visitors, the cost of entry, and the times when the function is due to start and finish. Almost certainly the licence will expire at least 30 minutes before your planned closing time.

Handing the bar over to a publican takes a load of work – and profit – off your shoulders; however, after a highly successful event some landlords will give you a donation towards the funds. There is no harm in asking outright about this when you make the booking And ask for a bottle of whisky for the raffle, too, while you are about it!

Frankly, to run a 'full' bar yourselves, you need someone in the team who has pub/club experience. Even then you will run into the problems not only of having to provide an enormous range of drinks – spirits, aperitifs, mixers, wines, beer, lager, cider and so on – but of being left with opened bottles at the end of the event. A nearly-full bottle of brandy or vodka is a very expensive commodity to get left with.

Most people coming to a money-raising event fully appreciate the difficulty of emulating hotel or pub facilities and are perfectly content with a choice of wine, beer, cider, soft drinks or whatever you decide you can offer. Dances, it seems, are an exception, and for some reason – perhaps to recharge the energy batteries – guests do seem to expect to be able to buy a little of whatever they fancy.

Shop around for the drink as carefully as you would for food. Prices vary enormously and if you are running the bar yourselves you will be under no obligation to buy everything under one roof. If you are tossing up between a wine merchant and a supermarket, take into account that your local wine merchant or off-licence will usually include free hire of glasses with a largish order and let you have the goods on sale or return, which is reassuring when you do not quite know your guests' capacity.

Not only that, a specialist will gladly guide you through his price list, pointing out the good buys, the wines that are most suitable for mulling, good 'mixers' – to use in wine cups – and so forth.

For party drinking by all means look at wines in 1-litre and 1.5-litre bottles, but bear in mind that the best bargains are often in standard 75-cl bottles. Cider is also sold in 2-litre bottles, and there is a scrumptious array of new brands; beer and lager are also in 2-litre non-returnable bottles, as well as in large cans. One thing I have learned about running even a simple bar is that people will come up and ask for what seems to me to be an obscure brand of their favourite tipple, express great disappointment that I do not have it, then knock back what I do offer them with a look of perfect contentment. The moral of this story is not to let the question of drink worry you too much.

When you are choosing wines to serve with a meal, either delegate the job to your friendly neighbourhood wine buff or make it a committee decision. When the wine is being bought on sale or return you can afford to offer a good selection in a wide price range, to sell by the glass or bottle. Your guests will feel flattered, and there will be nothing lost if they are not all sold. Simply return them with the crates of glasses.

Give non-alcoholic drinks careful thought. There is nothing more depressing from a non-drinker's point of view (I am told) than to be offered a sort of sickly-sweet orange squash they would not touch with a bargepole at home. Nor is there any excuse. Along with the usual orange, grapefruit and pineapple juices and the 'fizzies' (tonic water, bitter lemon and ginger ale), there is a wide and exciting range of less predictable alternatives. If a fruit grows on trees or bushes and is quaffable, you can bet your boots that someone has made a juice from it: they include apple juice, white or red grape juice (specially good spiced and mulled), guava, mango, blackcurrant and pear juices. In addition, there are all the sparkling spa waters, and the 'pretend' drinks such as non-alcoholic lager. Select one or two old faithfuls and one or two newcomers and you cannot go wrong.

Whichever job you get in the fund-raising stakes, it pays to imagine that the treasurer is sitting on your shoulder watching your every move; in the friendliest possible way, of course. When it comes to running a bar, he or she certainly should be. There is a statutory requirement to use 'standard measures' when serving spirits, beer and cider, but no such rule governs the serving of wine by the glass. It is absolutely vital, therefore, to decide whether you will pour six or eight glasses from a standard 75-cl bottle (proportionally more, of course, from the larger sizes), cost the wine accordingly and stick to it.

Problems arise when the amateur bar persons on duty change shifts after an hour or so, and someone with weak elbows becomes a bit too generous with the measure. Whoever is in overall charge of the bar must keep an eye on this aspect of the operation at all times.

If the price of your admission ticket is to include wine on the 'as-much-as-you-can-drink' basis, both costing the ticket and pouring the wine are acutely important. You will be the best judge of your own crowd, but reckon on half a bottle of wine per head at the minimum.

It is now obligatory to display a price list for all drinks to be purchased. As a general rule, beer and cider can be sold at a little above bar prices. Depending on the type of function, wine 'by the bottle' is usually sold at a mark-up of between 50 and 100 per cent on the cost price.

And what do happy bartenders have in their kitbag? Lots of ice, made weeks in advance by friends and stored in freezers; jugs of water, fruit juices, etc.; teatowels for wiping and polishing glasses (and enough pessimism to realize that the glasses may not be sparkling bright when they are delivered); cloths for wiping up spills; a bowl for on-the-spot washing-up; corkscrews that really work, crown cork openers and trays – lots of them; a 'float' of small change and a secure cash-box. Then there are the garnishes – oranges, lemons, sprigs of herbs – for which you will need a chopping board and knife; and a calculator, for when things get hectic.

The party may be over, but the work is not. As guests drift out on a 'high', saying what a marvellous time they have had and what wonderful value it all was, it is time for the clearing-up squad to move in. They have been volunteered well in advance, of course. The treasurer finds a quiet corner and quickly counts up the money from the various sources. No one can sleep until they have heard the provisional verdict. People who made puddings and pies claim their dishes; the old hands will have marked everything with their names. Furniture is packed away. The kitchen gets a spit and polish. Floors are swept. Glasses are washed up and packed in their boxes. Unsold drinks are stored in a safe place, ready to be collected.

And at the next committee meeting, the organizers will go over the event in detail, making a note of any aspect which could be improved upon, and reflecting whether there was enough food, or too much.

So much for this party: now on to planning the next.

In the pages that follow you will find, first, a guide to multiplying food quantities so that you can gauge how much you will need of the basic ingredients of your party fare. See also pages 98-100.

On pages 110-17 you will find a list of suggested party menus, ranging from the simplest drinks party or coffee morning to more extensive spreads, for both buffet-style meals and more formal entertaining. Always, when catering for a crowd:

(1) plan every detail, from menus and shopping to serving, well ahead;

(2) cut down the scale of the operation if your catering team is anything less than completely confident of being able to cope: no one expects *haute cuisine* on these occasions;

(3) avoid choosing dishes that will not wait, happily, until the hordes have assembled to consume them;

(4) avoid dishes that depend on last-minute attention – you almost certainly won't be in a position to give it;

(5) bear in mind that food will have to be transported; do this as far as possible in the containers in which it was cooked, and plan in advance what containers you will need for other items.

At-a-glance guide to multiplying up quantities

Ingredient/dish	25 portions	50 portions
Soup	4.6 litres/8 pints	9.2 litres/16 pints
Pâté	2 kg/4½ lb	3.6 kg/8 lb
Cold sliced meat	2.8 kg/6 lb	4.6 kg/10 lb
Boneless meat for casserole	3.6 kg/8 lb	6 kg/12½ lb
Turkey (oven-ready)	2 x 4 kg/9 lb birds	3 x 4.6 kg/10 lb birds
Chicken (oven-ready)	2 x 3 kg/6½ lb birds	4 x 2.8 kg/6 lb birds
Rice	1 kg/2¼ lb	1.8 kg/4 lb
Pasta	1 kg/2¼ lb	1.8 kg/4 lb
Vegetables, green or root (before preparing)	3.6 kg/8 lb	6 kg/12½ lb
Potato salad	1.4 kg/3 lb	2.3 kg/5 lb
Tomatoes	1.1 kg/2½ lb	1.8 kg/4 lb
Coleslaw: cabbage carrot walnuts mayonnaise	 700 g/1½ lb 225 g/8 oz 225 g/8 oz 300 ml/½ pint	 1.1 kg/2½ lb 400 g/14 oz 350 g/12 oz 450 ml/15 fl oz
Green salad: lettuce green peppers cucumber watercress	 3 large 2 2 2 bunches	 5 large 3 3 3 bunches
French dressing	300 ml/ ½ pint	450 ml/15 fl oz
'Paired' meringues: egg whites caster sugar soft brown sugar cream	 6 175 g/6 oz 175 g/6 oz 450 ml/15 fl oz	 12 350 g/12 oz 350 g/12 oz 900 ml/1½ pints
Soft fruit	3.4 kg/7 lb	6 kg/12½ lb
Fruit salad: mixed fruits, prepared weight syrup or fruit juice	 3 kg/6½ lb 1.5 litre/2½ pints	 5.2 kg/10½ lb 2.5 litres/4½ pints

Ingredient/dish	25 portions	50 portions
Cream, single or double	1 litre/1¾ pints	2 litres/3½ pints
French bread	3–4 sticks	5–6 sticks
Butter	25–40 pats	50–80 pats
Cheese (after a meal)	900 g/2 lb	1.7 kg/3½ lb
Cheese biscuits	900 g/2 lb	1.7 kg/3½ lb

SNACKS	Ingredients	Quantity
Sausage rolls	700 g/1½ lb flaky or shortcrust pastry 900 g/2 lb sausagemeat	30 medium 50 small
Vol-au-vents	900 g/2 lb flaky pastry 600 ml/1 pint thick white sauce 275 g/10 oz chopped prawns, mushrooms, etc.	50 small
Cheese straws	225g/8 oz cheese pastry (i.e. 225 g/8 oz flour, 100 g/4 oz butter)	80-100
Sandwiches	1 large loaf 25 small bridge rolls 150 g/6 oz butter *Choice of fillings:* 375 g/14 oz sliced cold meat 300 g/12 oz grated cheese 275 g/10 oz cream cheese 8 hard-boiled eggs, mashed 2 x 225 g/8 oz cans tuna fish or salmon, drained and flaked 1 medium cucumber, thinly sliced on a mandoline	12 rounds 25 whole, 50 halves

BEVERAGES

Coffee	275 g/10 oz ground coffee, or 75 g/3 oz coffee granules 3.4 litres/6 pints water 600 ml/1 pint milk 225 g/8 oz brown sugar	25 tea cups 50 coffee cups
Tea	50 g/2 oz tea 4.6 litres/8 pints water 1 litre/1¾ pints milk 225 g/8 oz sugar	25 tea cups

PARTY MENUS

Drinks Party

Lunchtime or early evening

Red, white and maybe rosé wines
Allow up to ½ standard (75-cl) bottle of wine per person.

Cloudy apple juice and spa water (mixed) with slices of lemon

Black grape juice

Serve red wine at room temperature (chilled if it is Beaujolais Nouveau); chill white and rosé wines and soft drinks.

Buy all drinks on sale or return. Hire glasses from wine merchant.

Grilled bacon rolls (with or without prunes inside): 2 each

Hot cocktail sausages on sticks: 2 each

Cheese straws: 4-5 each

Vol-au-vents or sausage rolls: 2 each

Nuts and crisps

Sherry Party

Lunchtime or early evening

Dry *fino*, medium *amontillado* and sweet 'cream' sherries
Pour 10–12 glasses from each standard (75-cl) bottle.
Allow 4-5 glasses each.

Cloudy apple-and-pear juice with slices of lemon

Lime juice and lemonade

Serve dry and medium sherries chilled, sweet sherry (which is very 'heavy' for lunch-time) at room temperature; soft drinks chilled.

Buy all drinks on sale or return. Hire glasses from wine merchant.

Cheese straws: 4–5 each

Nuts and crisps

Cheddar cheese and pineapple cubes on sticks: 2 each

Wensleydale or feta cheese and olives on sticks: 2 each

Cubes of salami and cucumber on sticks: 2 each

Cottage cheese and tomato dip: 350 g/12 oz for 25 people

'Dip-sticks' of carrot, green pepper, celery

Celery 'boats' filled with cream cheese and chopped walnuts: 2 each

Meze Party

Lunchtime or early evening (this is a drinks party with a Middle-Eastern flavour)

Greek or Cypriot white and red wines.
Allow up to ½ standard (75-cl) bottle per person.

Ouzo (an aniseed spirit)
Pour 20–24 measures from a standard (75-cl) bottle. Serve diluted with water. Allow 2 glasses per person (it is fairly powerful).

Serve white wine, ouzo, water and soft drinks chilled. Chill the red wine too, in summer.

Peach or apricot juice with spa water (mixed), with thin slices of lemon

Unsweetened orange juice with thin slices of orange

Buy all drinks on sale or return. Hire glasses from wine merchant.

Tzatziki (yoghurt, cucumber and mint dip)

Taramasalata (cods' roe pâté) bought from a delicatessen or supermarket delicatessen counter

Hummus (chick pea pâté)

Aubergine pâté

'Dip-stick' crudités: selection of green pepper, red pepper, cauliflower florets, cucumber

Fingers of hot *pitta* bread

Allow total of 700 g/1½ lb pâté for 25 people, and 6–8 crudités per person.

Cubes of feta cheese and black olives: 2 each

Small cold meatballs and cubes of cucumber on sticks: 2 each

Coffee Morning

Make ground coffee by the jug method (or use percolators and filters if you have enough), or make instant 'granules' coffee by the jug method. Allow 2 cups (200 ml/7 fl oz) each. For quantities see page 103.

Offer choice of decaffeinated coffee, tea and orange juice for any non-coffee drinkers.

Cheese scones, fingers of buttered banana and walnut teabread, fingers of orange 'tray-bake' cake, wholewheat shortbread biscuits
Allow 3–4 items each.

Strawberry Tea

Offer choice of Indian, China and a herb tea such as peppermint or camomile (which you can buy in tea-bag form). Allow 2 cups (200 ml/7 fl oz) per person.

Cucumber or egg and cress sandwiches: ½ round each

Strawberry tartlets decorated with a swirl of whipped cream: 1 each

Scones already topped (to avoid stickiness) with strawberry jam and whipped chantilly cream. (Make the cream go further by folding in beaten egg white.) Allow 1–2 each.

Sunday Brunch

Allow 2 cups of coffee each (see page 103), made with freshly ground coffee.

Tomato juice spiced with Worcestershire sauce, served chilled, with ice cubes and sprigs of mint: 1–2 glasses each
OR Buck's fizz (2 parts unsweetened orange juice to 1 part sparkling white wine): 2 glasses each

Cornets of thinly sliced ham filled with cream cheese and chopped green pepper or dates: 1 each

Scotch eggs: ½ each
OR Filled hard-boiled eggs: 2 halves each

Chicken drumsticks tossed in crumbs and baked: 1 each

Green salad

Hot French bread spread with garlic butter

Fruit cocktail of grapefruit segments (canned), orange or mandarin orange segments, sliced apple and melon cubes

Cheese and Wine Party

Lunch or evening

Buy a good selection of cheeses, a total of 2.3 kg/5 lb for 25 people. For example, farmhouse Cheddar, Leicester or Double Gloucester, Lymeswold, Stilton or Danish Blue, Edam or a smoked cheese, Camembert or Brie

Cheeses go further if you cut them into serving-sized pieces. However, crumbly ones such as Wensleydale resist such treatment.

Decorate the cheese boards with small bunches of black and white grapes, or with segments of tangerines or satsumas.

Offer a selection of celery sticks, gherkins, radishes, chicory leaves, watercress sprigs.

Butter
Allow 700 g/1½ lb for 25 people: it is much easier to buy ready-wrapped pats (which also prevent waste).

Choice of breads (black rye, wholewheat rolls, French sticks) and biscuits

Crisps and twig-biscuits

Cheese straws

Choice of red and white wines according to your price range and the price of the ticket
Choice of soft drinks

Choice of soft drinks

Pâté and Wine Party

Lunch or evening

Unless you have someone in your group who adores making pâté, buy a selection of pâtés in 2-kg/4½ lb dishes. Duck, pork and garlic, turkey, liver – they all come well garnished and looking very presentable. If the budget is very tight, cut them into serving-sized pieces and use the garnishes to decorate the serving plates. Allow 65–75g/2½–3 oz each, or 2 dishes for 40–50 people. (If, after buying in these quantities, you have any left over, buy it in to use later: it freezes perfectly.)

As a vegetarian alternative – also much cheaper – make mixed vegetable or mushroom pâté

Green salad tossed with orange segments

Bean salad, with 650 g/1¼ lb dried red kidney beans, chopped onion, garlic, peppers, herbs
OR Red cabbage and sweetcorn salad. Allow 800 g/1¾ lb cabbage and 350 g/12 oz sweetcorn kernels for 25 people.

Tomato salad

Choice of breads: black rye, pumpernickel, white cottage rolls, French sticks

Fresh apples and pears. Buy them by the tray. Allow slightly less than 1 piece of fruit each (not everyone will take one).

Dips and Dunks

Informal lunchtime or evening. Inexpensive. Popular with young people

Choice of dips

Cottage cheese, mashed banana, curry paste and chopped mango chutney

Cottage cheese, drained and flaked canned tuna, chopped red pepper, pinch of cayenne

Cream cheese, chives and chopped walnuts

Liptauer style, cream cheese and liver pâté with chopped green olives, gherkins and spring onions

Cream cheese, tomato paste, chopped skinned tomatoes, Worcestershire sauce, finely chopped leek

Allow total of 700–900 g/1½–2 lb dips for 25 people.

Celery 'boats' filled with liver pâté: 2 each

Cubes of pineapple, cucumber and olives on sticks: 2 each

'Dip-sticks', crudités of celery, carrot, red and green pepper strips, cauliflower florets, spring onions: 10–12 each

Choice of breads, such as French sticks, granary sticks, fingers of *pitta*, wholewheat rolls

Pitta and Kebab Party

Lunch or evening. Inexpensive. Popular with young people

Kebabs of cubed lean lamb, button onions (blanched in boiling water), button mushrooms, small tomatoes, bay leaves, prunes
Allow 2 x 15-cm/6-inch skewers each.

Kebabs of cubed collar bacon (soaked overnight), pineapple cubes, button onions, slices of green pepper
Allow 2 x 15-cm/6-inch skewers each.

Marinate kebabs for 1–2 hours in wine vinegar, oil and herbs.

Serve kebabs tucked into hot *pitta* and wholewheat *pitta* bread, or long white and wholewheat rolls.

Tomato sauce, pickles, relishes, lemon wedges to serve

'Kebab house' salad of shredded lettuce, thinly sliced onion, sliced green pepper, chopped mint

Greek, Cypriot or Turkish red and white wines, beer, lager and cider are all suitable accompaniments

Soup Kitchen

Lunch or evening. Inexpensive

Choice of 'blender' soups, carrot and orange juice, coriander and apple, curried parsnip, spinach and lemon

Serve swirled with single cream and topped with chopped herbs

Minestrone – buy canned consommé, stir in tomato purée and simmer julienne strips of carrot, celery and turnip and pasta shapes. Serve with grated cheese.

Puréed lentil soup (made with bacon stock) simmered with peas and sweetcorn kernels

If resources allow, serve bowls of croûtons, tiny bread cubes fried in butter. They can be frozen and re-heated in a low oven.

As soup is the 'main course' allow about 450 ml/15 fl oz per person

Jacket potatoes with plain yoghurt and grated cheese

Choice of farmhouse breads – cottage loaf, wholewheat, granary baps

Pie and Salad Party

Lunch or evening

Choice of cold 'double-crust' pies: chicken and ham; egg and bacon; fish, bacon and sweetcorn

Cornish pasties, vegetarian lentil and mixed vegetable pasties

Greek cheese or spinach and cheese pies made with *filo* pastry

Green salad of Chinese leaves and watercress

Tomato and onion salad

Dried fruit salad of apple rings, apricots, peaches, prunes. Allow 1.7–1.8 kg/3½–4 lb dried fruits for 25 people. Serve with plain yoghurt or soured cream.

Mexican Beano

Lunch or evening

Mexican rice with red and green peppers, chillis, canned pimento, *chorizo* spiced sausages
Allow about 900 g/2 lb rice for 25 people.

Chicken casserole with 3 x 1.6 kg/3½ lb chickens, peppers, onions and canned sweetcorn
OR Chilli beans with 1 kg/2¼ lb dried red kidney beans and 1.8 kg/4 lb minced beef for 25 people

Coleslaw

Green salad

Exotic fruit salad or oranges, grapes, canned pineapple dressed with a few sliced kiwi fruit or mangoes

Frozen cherry pie made with vanilla ice cream swirled with canned cherry pie filling on a crushed biscuit ('cheesecake') base
Allow 2.3 litres/4 pints ice cream and 800 g/1¾ lb pie filling for 25 people.

Curry Tiffin

Lunch or evening (strictly speaking, 'tiffin' means lunch)

Beef or lamb curry
Allow 4 kg/9 lb meat for 25 people. It is best made the day before and re-heated.

Potato curry
Allow 1.4 kg/3 lb potatoes for 25 people.

Rice

Side dishes of banana slices tossed in lemon juice and desiccated coconut, red and green pepper and onion rings, sultanas, chutneys

Grilled poppadoms: 1 each

Fruit salad: start it off with canned lychees

Buffet Lunch or Supper (cold)

Cold sliced turkey and ham
OR Coronation chicken with spiced apricot sauce
OR Lemon chicken

Vegetable salad of green beans and red peppers

Carrot, apple and walnut salad

Jacket potatoes or potato salad

Pickles and relishes with plain cold meats

Lemon or apricot mousse
Allow 450 g/1 lb dried apricots and 900 g/1½ pints cream for 25 people.

Red fruit salad of strawberries, redcurrants and raspberries

Cream

Buffet Lunch or Supper (hot)

Pork stroganoff
Allow 3.9 kg/8½ lb cubed lean pork and 450 g/1 lb button mushrooms for 25 people. The casserole is best made the day before and re-heated.

Rice

Broccoli spears
OR Green salad

Meringues, sandwiched with chantilly cream and chopped stem ginger or candied peel

Apple pies spiced with cloves

Cream

'Formal' Dinner

Leek and potato soup with chives, swirled with soured cream

White or wholewheat rolls

Beef bourguignonne
Allow 3.9 kg/8½ lb cubed lean beef for twenty-five people.

New potatoes or jacket potatoes

Petits pois

Baby carrots

OR play safe and serve mixed green salad

Apricot mille-feuille
Allow 3 x 350-g/12-oz packs frozen pastry for 25 people.

Cheese and biscuits

American 'Shower' Party

Lunch or supper. Bring-a-dish parties are popular in America, and a good idea for fund-raising as they spread the burden of the cooking. Ask everyone to make 8-portion dishes, to keep the calculating easy. Here are a few ideas:

Broccoli and cheese flan

Courgette, tomato and cheese casserole
Fish, prawn and red pepper quiche
Chicken and grape casserole
Vegetable risotto
Green pasta with chopped ham
Green salad
Lemon meringue pie
Pineapple and rice condé
Blackcurrant cheesecake
Strawberry mousse

Round-Robin Supper

Ask a dozen or so friends and neighbours (they have to live fairly close, for obvious reasons) to get together – and pay for the privilege! The group enjoys a single course at the first house and then moves on – and on.

First base: aperitifs such as dry sherry on the rocks, dry sherry and tonic water, vermouths (there is a long way to go!) and small, light snacks such as cheese bouchées

Second base: grilled kebabs of grapefruit and orange segments and soaked dried apricots marinated in orange juice, oil and herbs
OR Prawn, cucumber and fennel cocktail
Allow 350 g/12 oz prawns, 300 ml/11 fl oz sauce for 12 people.

Third base: chicken breasts stuffed with cheese and anchovies in white wine sauce
Potatoes baked in layers with onions and milk
Carrot 'pennies'
Whole green beans
Fourth base: hazelnut meringue gâteau with chocolate filling
Cheese and biscuits
Coffee

Pyramid Lunch

Another way to spread the load and enjoy a sociable occasion. One person, perhaps the campaign president or chairman, invites say 5 or 7 people to lunch – and collects an agreed amount. It is a matter of choice whether the host/hostess deducts the expenses. But what does need to be agreed is that the meals all along the line must be roughly similar – not caviar at one house and bread and cheese at the next.

Then each of the guests at the first party invites 4 or 6 people (depending on the original number: one less), and collects their money. They invite 3 or 5, and so on, until it comes down to a cosy *tête-à-tête* – and a big bag of money for the treasurer.

CHAPTER 9

Sales pitch

Generations of Britons have been content to be called a nation of shopkeepers, the implication being that if we were not running the corner newsagents, selling everything from a packet of beefburgers to a card of buttons, we would be behind the counter of a baby boutique at the smart end of town. I always felt that the saying was only partly true. An awful lot of people had never rung up a cash till in their lives . . . until recently. Now we *do* seem to be a nation of shopkeepers, stallholders, travelling salesmen, mail-order agents, telesales operators, wholesalers and swap-shoppers. And it's all going on in the name of charity.

Take last week, on a typical day in the office at home. The postman brought five envelopes. One of them was a letter asking me if I would run the bring-and-buy stall at a Café Continental, to raise money for our political association (I always do). Two were mail-order catalogues from the big national charities, with page after glossy page of Christmas cards, gifts, novelties and household goods – armchair shopping at its most comfortable and most beneficial.

The phone rang. The animal gloves I had ordered at an autumn bazaar – cats with their tongues sticking out and hedgehogs with snouty faces – were ready for collection. Oh, and would I like to sponsor a 41-year-old lady who was being rolled, wrapped up in her sleeping bag and a roll of thick carpet, from the railway station all the way to the shopping precinct and on to the pub (a good mile-and-a-half, I reckon)? The bazaar and this stunt were for the same cause, to amass a massive £60,000 for a heart machine in a new hospital wing; £18,000 had been raised already, but there was still a long way to go – some of it enveloped in the dubious comfort of a magic carpet!

There was a knock, and a cheerful little face appeared

over the top of the stable door: 9-year-old Catherine from next door, in uniform and with a basket over her arm, wanted to know if we would like to buy some biscuits. The Brownies had been given 30 pence each and asked to make it grow, to raise money for a children's day-trip to Belgium. She liked making biscuits, and thought other people might like eating them. One of her friends had spent the 'grow' money on washing-up liquid and was sprucing up all the cars in the vicinity, and another had bought odds and ends of ribbons and was making lavender and herb bags to sell. She would be coming round with them the following week.

Over a cup of coffee and one of Cathy's chocolate-drop biscuits, I flipped through the weekly booktrade magazine. 'Help raise £150,000 for Save the Children Fund's Famine in Africa Appeal' shrieked a headline. *The Children's Book*, an illustrated volume of verse, was now on sale. Seventy star celebrities had written the poems, 71 top illustrators had provided the artwork and the book had been typeset, published, promoted and distributed without a penny changing hands. Now it was the turn of the public. The book was in the shops, waiting for 75,000 charitably-minded customers.

The phone rang again. Jonathan, another neighbour's teenage son, who knew I was 'into health foods and things', was collecting on Christian Aid World Food Day and wanted to know if I had any packets of lentils, dried beans, rice or wholemeal flour to help the school fill fifty sacks. The food was to be delivered free by British Rail's Red Star service to London, then loaded on to two Band Aid container ships at Tilbury docks en route for Africa.

'If we can't quite manage to fill the sacks, we're going to have a jumble sale on Saturday and buy rice with the proceeds,' he explained, and rang off to work down his list of calls.

Making things, collecting things, selling things . . . the desperate need for money and food in disaster areas of the world and the increasing need for aid of all kinds in every community has made shopkeepers of us all, even if only for a day. We can all plug into the retailing business at any level we choose, whether it is selling pots of jam and geraniums at the garden gate or running a full-scale bazaar. As well as being all in a good cause, it's all enormous fun.

It is much *more* fun, of course, if you major on the things you do well, and enjoy doing. Harnessing your own special skills and those of your friends and neighbours is one of the golden keys to success.

Take a stall at the garden gate. There is something so homely and natural about these that they are almost impossible to resist. Many is the time I have screeched to a halt and come away with a bundle of leeks or a couple of cauliflowers when I already have a garden full of them. Everyone who has green fingers and a fertile little plot must have more produce than they know what to do with at some time of year. Maybe it would not occur to you to sell it and put the money into your own pocket. But if you sell it and put the money into a 'favourite cause' box, it soon adds up.

In an ideal world, perhaps, surplus food on any scale would be spirited away and delivered in perfect condition to the poor, hungry and needy parts of the world. Though that may not be practical, what *is* practical, if you live on a busy thoroughfare, is to weigh the produce in bags, tie it in bunches, put it in punnets, mark it clearly with the price, and have a money-box alongside labelled with the name of your chosen cause. You do need an element of faith. One of the saddest notices I saw was on a table outside a cottage in Kent, where cucumbers and early chrysanthemums were being offered for sale: 'Mr and Mrs Brown ask you please not to steal the money. It's for charity. Thank you.'

Without the necessary through-traffic to make a roadside stall a success, perhaps you could arrange to sell surplus crops to a local greengrocer (the label 'locally grown' always carries a certain cachet and makes an extra penny or two) or a weekly produce market?

There is not a ready sale, admittedly, for over-sized marrows, cooking pears and windfall apples, but these are the stuff that jams, jellies and chutneys are made of. Even taking into account the cost of sugar and spice and all things nice, plus your time, there is far more profit in pots of golden preserves glowing under pretty mob-caps of crisp cotton. Learn the trick of combining a 'glut' crop with one that is scarcer or more expensive. Marrow and plum jam, rhubarb and gooseberry, apple and elderberry jam, spiced pear and apricot 'cheese': not just apple jelly, delicious as it is, but apple and mint, rosemary, tarragon or thyme jelly if you have herbs in the garden as well, with a whole sprig of the aromatic leaves added for good looks and good measure.

Think of other sales outlets. There might be a craft shop nearby, or a pottery, or a shop selling home-made cakes, or tea-rooms, where pots of preserves would not be at all out of place. Explain that it is your way of turning overstocks into cash for a good cause, and the proprietor will surely be glad to do her bit, too.

One of the biggest growth industries in fund-raising – just about on a par with sponsorships – is the car-boot sale. This is despite the fact that the first posters which sprang up a couple of years ago were a complete mystery to half the people who saw them. Were they selling boots? In the summer? Not cars, certainly. Not car boots, either (though I actually heard one lady say that it was the first time she had realized that car boots were detachable, and could be sold separately). Then what? For the benefit of those just back from a prolonged visit to Outer Mongolia, I will explain: car-boot sales are portable garden-gate sales. If not enough potential customers pass your door to make it worth putting out a table of old radio parts or garden tools – or a mixture of both – or if the neighbours might not like it, then the mountain goes to Mahommed, and you take goods to the customers – in a car. You set up shop on an old trestle table or a door resting on a couple of piles of boxes, alongside a dozen or so of the nation's other nouveau shopkeepers, and reflect that Mr Marks and Mr Spencer started in a small way of business too. It is the greatest fun. No one feels intimidated – you could go to one and fill your own car boot for under a couple of pounds – yet there is always an air of expectancy. There could just be an Old Master lurking under a pile of comics on the next stall.

School playgrounds, community hall car parks, village greens, spacious gardens, the drive leading up to the church – all these have played host to this first-timer's way of playing shops. The sale is easy as pie to organize –

you just get together with a group of colleagues or committee members – and for most venues there will be no expenses at all. Children's toys, books and comics, outgrown clothes, tools, china and household goods, that old pair of curtains that faded in the wash – it is amazing what attention and interest they all command. There is just one problem: like so many good ideas, the car-boot sale is in danger of suffering from over-exposure. If your area seems to have had one practically every weekend since you can remember, it could be the shrewdest thing to give it a rest.

Car-boot sales are outdoor jumble sales by another name, in fact. It will take another generation or so to see whether they will completely supersede the good old-fashioned free-for-all sale in the town hall, or whether the two so-similar events will continue to flourish side by side. For the time being, at any rate, I am happily able to report that the jumble sale is alive and well, and it seems as good a way as any to make £50 or £60 in a couple of hours.

Do not be fooled by the humble nature of the event into thinking it is not worth advertising. To my mind, it is not worth holding one if you do not let people know about it. How otherwise are you going to attract the JSF (jumble sale fraternity) in your neighbourhood? Every locality has them, the people who are there a good half-hour before the doors are due to open, huge shopping-bags at the ready and clutching a copy of a little grey pocket book listing silver hallmarks and date letters. Armed with this they can go straight to the white elephant stall and, certain they have a bargain, pick up a discarded item or two of someone's family silver. They will not be able to do that if you are smart, though. Shrewd JSOs (organizers) invite a reliable antique dealer to have a look round once everything is set out, and make an offer for any items of special value.

There is a JSS (specialist) in every community. She is the lady who collects up the jumble, stores it in a garage or shed – for not all of it will have come straight from the dry cleaner's – and sorts it out. That is how you get separate stalls for children's clothes; 'nearly new' clothes, or at least those that have some sartorial possibilities in the future;

patchwork corner, where almost anything goes (I know a lady who made a patchwork quilt entirely out of simulated fur she had picked up at sales); and lucky dip, anything in this box – which did not sell when it was put out at the last sale – a penny. That is the box to offer to the rag dealer who will come round while you are packing up. For even with jumble there does come a time when some items are definitely surplus to future requirements. Too much 'real' jumble doing the rounds at sale after sale is not good for appearances, or profit.

Too much high-class stuff is not all that beneficial either. The JSF do not on the whole go to sales with bulging wallets, so if you happen to have been given a couple of Italian suits with designer labels, this is not the market-place for them. Save them for a nearly-new sale, or organize a coffee or sherry morning at someone's house and run a swap shop as a sideline.

It is thirsty work, running and attending jumble sales. You should definitely offer customers a cup of tea and a cake, and have cake and produce stalls too, to attract a different type of trade.

Several charity sales throughout Britain welcomed a happy band of willing teamakers as part of the Brownie scheme to make and sell one million cuppas. Teabags were donated by a generous importer and the girls found their own sales pitches – jumble and car-boot sales, old people's homes, hospital visiting hours, fire stations, building sites, tourist spots, anywhere a nice hot cuppa and a merry smile would be welcome. The Brownies charged 10 pence a cup. Significantly, this is all it costs to keep one starving child in Africa alive for one day.

Oxfam shops, happy hunting grounds for clothes, basketware, stationery and gifts in so many towns and cities, have shown how very successful shopkeeping-for-a-day can be, as in many cases they are run by part-time staff on a rota system. Be on the look-out for sales possibilities for your favourite cause. A shop that has been vacated and has only a short lease to run, perhaps one which is due for later demolition under a reconstruction scheme, could present a good sales outlet for 'nearly new' and gift items: high-class jumble, in other words. You do need to apply for planning permission, but all things being equal the request will surely be given favourable consideration.

We had enormous fun running a 'town hall' shop in the village where I used to live. The committee had found that it was too strapped for cash to carry out the necessary repairs. Panic! Then someone offered us the use of an old bakery in the high street, we had a clearing-up party (headscarves and yard brooms the order of the day), put up notices and asked door to door for white elephants and produce to sell – posh jumble and jams, we used to say. Junk jewellery (always on the brink of coming back into fashion), pickling jars, table lamps, books that could still teach most of us a thing or two, baskets brimming over with D'Arcy spice and Bramley apples – we collected enough to encourage an orderly and impatient queue to form outside on opening day. Some people donated their goods outright, others wanted a share of the takings (this made less profit for the cause, of course, but more fun for the sales staff). A woman came in with a set of saucepans, a snakeskin handbag and a hard-luck story: if we could only sell these for her she would have enough for the airfare for a summer holiday. It was at times like that when we pulled out the stops (sales conference lecturers would have been proud of us), and proved that there is a super-salesman lurking deep inside even the most timid of us. Yes, the lady went to Spain, and still the town hall benefited. With the proceeds from the shop, a flourishing covenant scheme, a dance and other functions it got its new roof *and* a lick of green paint into the bargain.

Working as a team, whether it is selling things or making things to sell, is part of the fun of fund-raising – and indeed what attracts some people to get on the band-wagon in the first place. For every person who is so rushed off her feet she does not know which way to turn, there are two or three, probably living in the same street, who are just longing to join in the activity, do something useful and feel needed. Making things to sell is a marvellous way of harnessing people's time and willingness, and of bringing new friends and neighbours into the hub of the community. Usually it only takes one enthusiast to start the ball rolling and get people organized. After that there is no stopping them.

One such leading light in our locality had the ambitious notion of turning a condemned and tumbledown thatched cottage into an agricultural museum, and making it the headquarters of the historical society. The village had not seen activity like it since the days of horse fairs along the high street and sheep fairs on the green, when every other house – ours included, apparently – hung a bough over the front door to show that it was licensed to sell liquor for the day. Several summer dances, picnic lunches, turkey suppers in the town hall, donation appeals and a lot of hard work later, the museum was flourishing – as a school.

We used to rush home from work in the evening, dash across the road and take our places in front of the log fire to learn how to make corn dollies. 'It doesn't matter what you do. It'll never turn out right unless you select your straw,' the old farmworker-cum-craft-instructor impressed indelibly on our minds, so much so that soon we were all able to make Essex cornucopias, Hertfordshire lanterns, Cambridgeshire bells, Staffordshire knots and Welsh fans that looked a treat hanging from the oak timbers, and sold like hot cakes. And they were not cheap, either.

Another craftsman came with bundles of rushes, troughs to soak them in and a good line of patter which he kept up while 15 or so pupils fumbled their way through the growing pains of the intricacies of basketwork. Table mats, plant-pot holders, bowls and, the ultimate triumph, lidded baskets were eventually produced, and sales to the weekend visitors went a long way towards the upkeep of the museum.

Fired with enthusiasm, and always willing to crib an idea, we invited the group to go on meeting every week for ages afterwards in our kitchen (we had resilient brick floors), and had a fascinating line-up of tutors. Pooling our ideas and capabilities, we made dried-flower arrangements, acorn necklaces, seed collages, string pictures, slab pottery, Christmas-tree ornaments – anything, in fact, that could be achieved without recourse to a needle – and the results furnished many a bazaar stall.

I looked in on a group like this the other day in Dunmow, home of the flitch trials, where a dozen or so ladies were being taken step by step through the manufacture of Christmas crackers. Here is an 'all-things-to-all-persons' hobby for you. Someone with an eye for a bargain goes round at sale time buying up ends of lines (sets of earrings, screwdrivers, key-rings, nail clippers, bracelet charms and the like) for the presents. Someone with a contact at a proper cracker factory gets a good deal on the bangers, hats and jokes; without such a lead you can easily buy them wholesale from a novelty firm (page 160). The jokes come in big sheets, some more suited to family entertainment than others, and you cut them up. Can you imagine solemnly sitting down and writing them? Someone with an eye for design buys the high-tension crêpe paper (cheap kinds will not do: they tear long before you get them to crinkle), sequins, sequin sheet off-cuts, ribbons, motifs, braid and fancy papers for the decoration. And someone else makes sure there is an ample supply of the cheapest possible grey card for the foundation.

Then it is action time. Everyone brings his or her own scissors, stapling machines, pencil and rulers, and starts preparing the various items: piles of card precision-cut to two sizes, stacks of red, green and white crêpe paper (someone thinks blue would be nice for a change), bundles of silver and gold ribbons just long enough to tie in bows – the raw materials build up. And so, at the end of it all, do the profits. The crackers were sold for £1 each at a Christmas bazaar, one of many ventures stretching over several years to earn what it takes to convert a building in Chelmsford, Essex, into a much-needed hospice.

Whether it is novelties for crackers, hollow straw for corn dollies or fake fur to edge dolls' capes, it always pays to ask around to see if someone knows someone who can supply it cheaply or, better still, would be prepared to donate it. Manufacturers' warehouses must be lined with end-of-range or slightly damaged items that are virtually valueless to them, and like gold dust to bazaar-stall organizers. If you can find a local source of supply to tap, so much the better. A letter to a firm stressing that certain facilities are urgently needed in your town, or what a group in your county is doing to raise funds for a disaster appeal, is likely to fall on more fertile ground.

Ideas are what fund-raising is all about. Sow the seeds of a good idea, get people enthusiastic and the job is half done. Sometimes the ideas will be sparked off by a ready supply of some particular material: a mill not far from us was the source of bags of nylon off-cuts in red, white and blue polka dots, a sometime flavour-of-the-month which blossomed into gifts, toys, dolls' clothes and household goods enough to furbish a large red, white and blue bazaar stall. The colour co-ordination made sense from the customers' point of view, too – the frilly aprons matched the potholders which matched the place-mats which matched the teddy-bears' waistcoats.

Colour themes are good news for stalls. The overall design chooses itself, and the whole effect could not be more eye-catching. One of the most stunning I ever saw (inspired perhaps by Cecil Beaton's costumes for the film version of *My Fair Lady*?) was a black and white stall. A crisp white cloth covered the trestle table, alternating strips of black and white crêpe paper were wound round the supports and a striped sheet formed a canopy over the top, the whole ensemble resembling a candy-striped four-poster.

Someone's local mill somewhere must have had a spring-clean, we noticed, for the same black and white fabric designs cropped up over and over again, in checked gingham covers for pots of preserves and pâté, dolly-bags filled with dried rose petals, braid-trimmed semi-circular place mats, pierrot dolls, pencil cases, cosmetic bags, babies' bibs and jokey stuffed animals with red cummerbunds: and in a dash-and-slash abstract design for cushion covers, picnic tablecloth-and-napkin sets and padded boleros. Add a splash of colour and the theme goes merrily through a Noah's ark of knitted animals – zebras with yellow eyes, cats with red bow ties, elephants with green scarves and monkeys with blue hats.

Even food was in evidence: gingerbread, Christmas puddings and fruit cakes as near black as could be, sponge cakes and cookies with frosty white icing, and covered candy boxes with melt-in-the-mouth sugar fondants – it was quite a stall.

A 'tuck shop' has a certain *je ne sais quoi* to it that makes it even more appealing than a sweet stall. You need to get everyone saving glass coffee and other jars, date boxes and see-through chocolate boxes from day one, when the decision is taken. They will never manage to collect enough, though, so buy pressed paper or clear plastic beakers in bulk to use as containers. Fudge cut up in squares, chewy toffee, chocolate-covered peanuts, pink, green and white coconut ice and raspberry truffles all look good in beakers covered with cling-wrap or, more prettily, crackly transparent paper tied round with ribbons.

Tall jars, flat boxes and compressed paper or trays are good for finger-licking sticks of shortbread, flapjacks, date slice and sesame bars. Do not forget that the wind of change is blowing as surely through the tuck shop as it is through the supermarket, and children nowadays are healthily into muesli bars, honey and sunflower-seed bars and the like. Samosas do a brisk trade at a 'real' school tuck shop I know.

Some goodies – Paddington-shaped ginger biscuits, rice crispie chews and sugar mice – are not worth giving fussy wrappings. They are just too tempting, and you know from experience they will never make it to the door.

Have you ever heard of a mouse-ometer? It is a new kind of opinion poll. They had one in the window of a home-made cake shop just before the General Election. A customer supplied the shop with sugar mice in blue, red and orange to be sold in aid of charity as election 'favours'. The saleslady moved the hands on the appropriate segment of a cardboard clock each time she sold one. It was not quite as accurate – or maybe it was – as a national opinion poll, but it created a lot of interest locally and raised quite a bit of money.

When it comes to selling things, I am all in favour of gimmicks. We had an 'Owl and the Pussy-cat' stall once. Needless to say, the inevitable trestle table was got up to look as much like a beautiful pea-green boat as possible. Then everything, but everything, depicted our two animal heroes in some way. The stall organizer wrote to greetings card, calendar and stationery firms with a heart-felt plea for any left-overs, and I am still writing thank-you notes on barn-owl cards to this day.

She drew up standard owl and cat soft-toy patterns, and

helpers made them up in any size and any material, giving them what accessories they liked. We had cats on their way to market with little straw baskets, others on their way back carrying bunches of flowers, owls sweeping with yard brooms and others reading books. She bought knitting patterns and handed them out, with skeins of donated wools, to a senior citizens' group, who interpreted the designs with as much humour as Edward Lear had put into his poem. And she bought sheets of transfers which went on to 'ordinary' things, to keep them in the fold. That market, with that stall, must have been nearly ten years ago, and people still talk about it – and adapt the idea – even now. That owl and that pussy-cat between them had bred a mouse stall, a rabbit stall and a hedgehog stall – not exclusively pincushions and almond-studded cakes – to my knowledge.

In a more romantic vein, we had a Floral Bouquet stall which was roses, roses (and other blossoms) all the way, in pretty cotton materials, embroidered motifs, dried-flower posies. pressed-flower bookmarks, water-colour miniatures, cake decorations, little boxes of candied primroses, saffron buns, dried camomile flowers for tea, and rose-petal jelly – also for tea. This stall had the sweet smell of success even before it opened for business.

The success of any sales operation is almost totally dependant on one thing: pitching the price right. It should not be too high, otherwise everyone who comes to the shop or stall will go away with that polite, glazed 'just looking' expression that sales assistants dread. Nor should it be too low: that is potential profit going out of the window.

You have to make an assessment. Think of the general run of the customers you aim to attract. If they were not buying the presents and the preserves from you, where would they be buying them? In a top-people's shop? A supermarket? In the street market? If you can get a 'feel' about their normal buying habits, however rough a generalization it may be, you will have a fair idea of the range of prices they will be prepared to pay.

You also have to take into account the prices of comparable goods in comparable places, plus the cost of materials, then make an allowance for the time spent. People cannot and do not expect to get something for nothing, but equally they are unlikely to pay top craftsmen's rates for a stocking present for Auntie.

Never be afraid to ask advice – from other people who have run stalls and bazaars in your area, and from real shopkeepers. Yes, you are in competition with them, but not regularly; how could they mind?

While you are there asking the professionals for their advice, do not forget to ask them if they would like to have a collecting box on the counter, a poster in the window, or would be willing to donate a prize for the raffle (the cheek of Old Nick, my grandmother used to call it).

The last word on sales appeal must be fund-raising by brand image. It is not every day you can gaze into Paul Newman's flashing blue eyes – or at least, it used not to be until Newman allowed his photograph to be used on a salad-dressing label. There is nothing special about the oil and vinegar in Newman's Own, but something quite special about the packaging. Sales raised £3.3 million when the product was launched in the United States and Australia, and it is now available in Britain too. Most special of all, the entire profits from this product go to charities selected by the actor. Whoever had *that* idea certainly knew what the power of a famous face can achieve.

STALLS IN BRIEF

Looking for ideas? Close your eyes, stick a pin in one of these, and see if it appeals.

Easter-egg stall (for a spring fair)

Stock it with painted, dyed, spatter-sprayed, sequinned and braided hard-boiled eggs; plain eggcups decorated to match, or with pressed flowers 'painted' over with melted wax; egg-shaped candles made inside blown eggshells; tiny painted egg-shell vases to fill with spring flowers (provide cardboard egg boxes for safe transportation home); egg cosies.

Marzipan eggs and fruit; chocolate eggs; cardboard eggs filled with home-made sweets and chocolates; scotch eggs; hot cross buns; simnel cakes; Easter cakes; butterfly and other fancy cakes.

Felt, fabric and knitted rabbits, chickens and ducks, including some with Easter bonnets.

Pots with flowering bulbs – daffodils, tulips, crocuses (remember to plant early for Easter); *pots et fleurs* – pots planted with evergreens such as ivy, and spring-flowering plants; margarine tubs filled with moss and arrangements of spring flowers.

Kitchen corner

Frilly and practical aprons; covers for eggcups, teapots, coffee pots, mixers and food processors; place-mat, table-cloth and napkin sets; hand towels cut from towelling lengths and edged with braid. Knitted dishcloths and floor cloths; felt or fabric hold-all bags to tidy away plastic bags, polishing cloths, dusters and the like; felt or fabric hanging bags with deep pockets for freezer pens and ties, wooden spoons, etc.; gingham-covered seat cushions with ties.

Wooden wall racks for bottles and jars; wooden string holders; brightly painted coffee and similar jars and cocoa and similar tins, for storage; sets of inexpensive jars (from chemists' suppliers) filled with dried herbs.

Pots of herbs for the windowsill; bunches of dried herbs; wire hoops (from bent coathangers) covered with dried bay, rosemary and other evergreen herbs (admire now, eat later); bouquet garni sachets in jars, tins or on hanging ropes.

Bathroom beauty

Pretty cosmetic, soap and sponge bags and pouches; braided hand-towel-and-face-cloth sets; padded neck cushions; shower caps; towelling slip-on slippers.

Towelling hang-it-alls with pockets for plasters, bandages and tubes of cream (not to be used for medicines and tablets); hanging holders for air fresheners; loo-roll holders – every design from crinoline ladies to full-blown chrysanthemums; tiny guest soaps and bath salts in painted and decorated jars.

Tall, narrow boxes (made by the handymen in the

group) to conceal loo brush, cleanser, etc.; wooden towel rails.

North Pole stall

Everything for chilly weather – ideal for a Christmas fair: woolly hats, gloves, scarves, mitts, legwarmers, socks, bedsocks, shawls, knee rugs, sweaters, cardigans; fun-fur hats; muffs; ear-muffs; cravats and slippers; hot-water bottle covers; thick, ribbed tights (if you can buy them cheaply).

Eskimo dolls – some with fishing rods; wrapped-up-well dolls of all kinds with fur or woolly hats, muffs, capes, leggings.

Felt appliqué or patchwork thermometer pencil-cases, spectacle cases or make-up bags with the mercury showing a below-freezing temperature.

London Town stall

Absolutely anything shaped like a great big red London bus, from a felt knitting bag to a pincushion to a pencil-case to a place-mat to a nursery rug; knitted policemen, Beefeaters and guardsmen (you can buy the patterns for these toys); London-scene tins, beakers and mugs (which you can buy cheaply) filled with home-made sweets, cookies and biscuits; plain T-shirts decorated with 'London' transfers (you can buy ones with historical buildings, maps of the Underground and so on); sweaters, gloves and other knitted items with bus and Tower of London-type motifs.

Chelsea buns, currant buns, sticks of London rock, bus-shaped iced biscuits, bus-stop lollipops. It's an eye-catching logo!

Bluebell stall

According to an old adage, 'blue and green should ne'er be seen', but the colours do make a compelling partnership. Combine knitted and sewn items in blue and/or green – they are both good colours for kitchen, bathroom or bedroom.

In the toy section, possibilities include frogs, exotic fish and birds, knitted nurses in uniform, policemen, children in school uniform, pixies.

Indoor plant cuttings in tiny pots – scented geraniums, ivy, fuchsia, or whatever your green-fingered circle can provide; posies and bunches of dried flowers (long sprays of bells of Ireland, delphinium and larkspur, clusters of dried cornflowers, statice, alchemilla mollis); dried seed-heads dyed subtle shades of blue and green; pots of blue hyacinths, crocus and other spring-flowering bulbs.

Tablecloths, place-mats, napkins, bibs and tuckers embroidered with a bluebell motif – fortunately an easy one to draw – and enamelled tin plates painted in enamels with bunches of bluebells or a bluebell-wood scene copied from a greetings card.

Teddy-bears' picnic stall

This could be the all-time winner. Teddy-bear shops are sweeping America, where soon every self-respecting town will have one, and are now invading the UK. Bears of fake-fur, felt, other fabric and knitted wool can never fail to find friends. Some of our favourite ursine friends from the nursery are copyrighted, but close relations are permitted. Once you have a standard pattern, make families of bears – grannies, aunts, uncles, sisters and cousins; some can be holding baby bears, suitcases, pots of marmalade, jars of honey, bacon sandwiches, or any of the other items bears are known to treasure.

Children's clothes – scarves, mittens, slippers, sweaters – with bear motifs are sure-fire sellers, and you can transform plain pottery pencil-holders, plain tin pencil-boxes, wooden boxes, cardboard wallets, recycled stationery – anything that is cheap, cheerful and plain – by using stick-on bear transfers, which you can buy by the strip.

Lastly, do not forget the edible teddies: bear-shaped biscuits, gingerbread, parkin and shortbread will appeal to children from nine months to 90 years old.

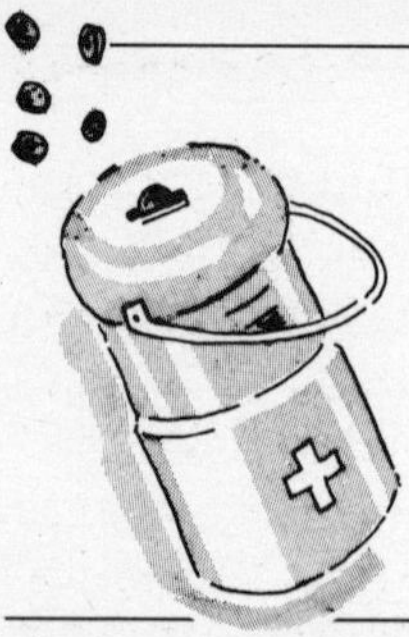

CHAPTER 10

The money game

Pennies in a jar; pounds in a piggy bank; a cheque from the company secretary; a long-term deed of covenant – supporters pay their money and take their choice how they pay it. It is just as well that some largish capital sums are raised for charities without teams of people hop-scotching from one end of the land to the other on a sponsored kangaroo trek. The roads would get so awfully crowded.

On the principle that 'great oaks from little acorns grow', small amounts of money, however collected, are just as welcome as large donations from wealthy benefactors. There is always the chance that someone who drops a coin into a box on the counter in the dry cleaner's and reads the charity's message will want to know more.

Pubs and shops are marvellously co-operative in this kind of venture. The collecting boxes for national charities all have ready-printed labels. Some go further, with articulated toy scenes which make it positively compelling to roll a coin down a chute and make the monkeys swing from branch to branch or the drummer-boy do his stuff. If you want to support a national organization in this coin-in-the-slot way, write to its headquarters; they will send you the appropriately labelled containers, and you can then approach tradespeople to place them in high-density situations.

The idea, simple though it is, works equally well for local ventures, too. A huge glass jar with a neatly written label clearly stating the aim of the collection – the playing field, the cinema restoration fund, a bus-shelter or whatever – can clock up quite a tidy sum in small change, particularly in a club or pub on party night. For safety's sake, make it the largest jar that has ever been made, and position it where it is never out of sight. A village publican I know had just counted his 'takings', filled in a bank paying-in slip and put them back safely in the jar when he turned his back on the bar. The jar disappeared, and so did £389. He tore up the bank slip, put a fiver in another bottle and started all over again. I think he said 'Blast'.

There is no law to stand between you and a coin collection as long as it is for a good cause. It is illegal to collect for personal gain – however worthy a cause that may seem at times. And it is certainly advisable to ask for a receipt from the bank or charity treasurer acknowledging your donation. There is quite an art in the oversize receipt/cheque business nowadays, and a huge Monopoly-money type of cheque that can be framed and read at twenty yards distant draws attention to the fact that another collection is already in progress. If the charity does not have its own printed monster cheques and receipts, maybe one of your number could draw one up. They make very good props for publicity photos and televised presentations.

Some social clubs and pubs – presumably those frequented by architects, builders and other clients with a steady hand – build piles of pennies, or miles of pennies. (Someone with a calculator works out that if all the coins in the pile were placed edge to edge in a line it would take a long time to walk from one end to the other.) Eventually the time comes when the penny pyramid gets so high, you could knock it down with a feather. The publican puts on a party hat, all the regulars turn up, there is an on-the-spot competition to guess the value, four stalwarts hold out a blanket and someone gives a very gentle shove in the right direction. It is the money-making equivalent of demolishing a factory chimney, and about as nerve-wracking. Who would have thought you could build an edifice over four feet high and top the £250 mark before the day of reckoning?

Pubs in our area – where air force bases are thick on the ground – have other ways of relieving people of their small change. They have set up a scheme to encourage American servicemen returning to the States to turn out their pockets, purses, boxes and drawers and leave the pence and pounds behind them for charity. It is nothing for a lieutenant cheerfully to wave goodbye to £60 or £70 before he boards the plane. Such a gesture shows great public spirit, particularly as the donor will not even be around to see the outcome of his generosity.

House-to-house collections, well established for the British Legion Poppy Day and other household names among the charities, need careful orchestrating for local appeals. As a nation, we are suspicious of callers, and as a collector you have to be prepared for quite a few rejections, too, particularly if you are covering a heavily-worked street (often those residential roads nearest the centre of town). When a friend of mine refused to buy a cheap ballpoint pen from a charity collector she was actually sworn at: what the caller did not know was that he was the third within an hour to knock at that particular door, and generosity had worn thin by that point.

Of course, it helps if you see the situation from both sides. For all the occupier knew, he could have been facing his twentieth rejection in a row, his shoes may have been letting in water, and he may have been missing the Cup Final on television . . . Still, that was no excuse for him to swear at a potential customer.

If you do decide to have a house-to-house collection, have a box or tin with a clear label, and carry a letter of authority from the object of your endeavours – the hospital, chairman of the village hall committee and so forth. To be honest, I do not recommend it. I feel there are other, more convivial, ways of helping you to rake in the shekels at a local level, as you will know now from reading earlier chapters of this book.

Sitting with your hand out waiting for the money to come in may sound like someone's idea of Heaven. It is. And it works. Many churches have found that an appeal letter from the parish priest drawing attention to the increasing expense of maintaining the building – the state of the roof, or the need for repairs to the heating system (always close to the congregation's heart) – has gratifying results. The cleric, having stated his case, nominates a day when he will be in the church ready to receive his flock and their gifts. People who might not have responded to an envelope appeal seem to welcome this opportunity for an informal chat, and turn up in encouraging numbers, to hand over a cheque or a sealed donation.

The idea must be worth a try for other organizations, too. What about asking a local personality, elected councillor or council official to play host and receive the money in the village hall, the school pavilion, the hospital wing or whatever? Curiosity and the chance to chat to a 'name' can reach purses that other appeals might not reach.

Organizations which need to raise money in a big way, for large capital expenditure and heavy running costs – a private hospice, for example – have to delve deeply and professionally into ways of money-gathering. Not for them a leaning tower of pennies. There are tricks of the trade here and lessons to be learned which can benefit appeals of all kinds and at every level.

As for so many kinds of selling – and an appeal for funds *is* selling something: a message – a mailing list is invaluable. If you are raising funds for a political party, you will have your membership cards and a record of all those who pledged support at the last election, or when the last survey canvass was carried out in the area. If the aim is to build a new science laboratory, or improve the changing facilities and the swimming-pool at the school, then there are parents and past pupils to be contacted. One of the purposes, it seems to me, of having an old girls' or an old boys' association is not so much so that they can get together periodically and pat each other on the back as that there is a constantly updated record in the secretary's office of changes of names and address: the very stuff that mailing lists are made of!

If you are starting from scratch, without this natural nucleus of known interest, you will have to build up your own list (unless you buy a list, or part of a list, from a mail-order house or agency, but this will be expensive – so much for one thousand names – and wasteful; not everyone who buys furniture or luggage by post or goes on Continental holidays is going to be sympathetic to your appeal.)

Get a copy of the electoral register from the local council and there you have, street by street, the names of residents who might support a community appeal. Go through the *Yellow Pages* or other local telephone registers and extract names of businesses in the locality, then telephone each one to ask the name of the chairman or managing director. Go to a large library and ask for a copy of a management register – there is one which lists the top 10,000 companies in Britain, which is handy, if you happen to live in a highly industrialized area – and glean what information you can about who runs the big businesses locally. Armed with this ammunition – the names as well as the addresses – you can fire your first salvo: a letter.

How you angle this letter will depend of course on the scale of your operation and the size of your target, but there are general guidelines which are universal. First and foremost, do not be apologetic: no 'I'm sorry to trouble you but . . .' nonsense. *You* know the money is vitally needed and will be put to good use. Say so. State your targets in material terms (what services or facilities you hope to provide) and in cash terms (how much you need to raise). Say by what other means you intend to raise the money (to show how hard everyone is working). And be as open about the project as possible.

If you are raising the money to build and maintain a hospice, invite the 'big guns', any well-known or well-connected local people and those in a fair way of business, to come to see the building before conversion and examine the plans.

When there is a lot at stake – and in the case of hospices, the capital sum needed can run into well over £1 million – invite a small selection of people to a series of buffet lunches or drinks receptions. Ask the architect or designer to make a presentation of the plans and a doctor to describe the facilities. No one needs to be convinced of the need for a hospice in the community, but many people will have absolutely no idea of the cost of providing and maintaining one. Almost without doubt, someone on your committee or one of the trustees will donate the refreshments on such occasions.

Invite individuals to make a donation by cheque, and when they do, make a point of acknowledging the gift immediately, with an appropriate paragraph about the specific way in which the donation will help. Keep a card index file, or any other system you find convenient – large organizations now use computers, of course – and follow up the donation a year later with an 'anniversary letter', setting out what has been achieved in the past twelve months and what still remains to be done. Experience shows that in 20 per cent of cases this will bring in a further donation, often larger than the first. Once they have donated to an appeal, and now have news of the work in progress, people feel comfortable with the cause, like one of the family. Your good cause has become their concern too.

To keep the money flowing in annually, invite well-wishers to sign a banker's order form. Large charities have them printed with the name and number of their bank accounts, and you can do the same. Ask your bank manager for advice: he will have a form to show you as an example. Donors fill in the forms pledging a specific sum to be paid at intervals (monthly, quarterly, half-yearly or annually) and send the forms to you. You extract the information, itself a boon for forward planning and budgeting, and send the form on to the donor's bank.

A deed of covenant is even more advantageous, since it carries specific tax exemption. Anyone who pays tax at the standard rate or above finds this a very satisfying way of making a donation because, thanks to the generosity of the taxman, the charity receives more money than the donor actually pays.

It works like this. The donor fills in a form pledging a specified sum for a minimum of four years, or up to ten years, and, together with a banker's order to that effect, forwards the form to the charity. It is then up to the charity to present the forms to the Inland Revenue and recover the exempted tax; incidentally, tax is always repaid at the standard rate, even if the donor pays tax at a higher rate.

The table overleaf shows how beneficial this means of payment is. The figures are correct at the time of writing, but will of course vary if the standard rate of income tax is changed:

Deeds of covenant			
Gift	The Appeal recovers basic rate income tax at 30%	The gift to the Appeal is worth	Over 4 years gift is worth
£10 a month	£51.43 a year	£171.43 a year	£685
£5 a month	£25.72 a year	£85.72 a year	£343
£4 a month	£20.58 a year	£68.58 a year	£275
£3 a month	£15.43 a year	£51.43 a year	£206
£2 a month	£10.29 a year	£34.29 a year	£137
£1 a month	£5.15 a year	£17.15 a year	£69

Of course, to qualify for this concession the organizers of any appeal must satisfy the Inland Revenue that the cause comes within the specific – but broad – definition of a charity. As defined by the Revenue for this purpose, that is any organization collecting funds for the benefit of children, education, those who are mentally or physically ill, the disabled, the aged and the poor, for example. Specifically excluded (it goes without saying) are profit-making organizations and fund-raising for personal gain in any shape or form.

The Revenue does not smile benignly on donations to a political party. These do not qualify for tax relief, except in the case of advertisements in a brochure, newsletter or leaflet published by the party organization. Shopkeepers and other business people who take space in publications of that kind may enter the cost against tax.

As always, it is a case of asking for advice if you are in doubt. Talk to your local tax inspectors: one of their main functions, I have it on the highest authority, is to advise, and they certainly show a sympathetic understanding in all money matters relating to charity.

It might sound too good to be true, but if you are raising money for a registered charity, a donation could be there for the asking. There is a group of trust funds, administered by the Charities Aid Foundation (address on page 160) which has money for disbursement to approved organizations. The Foundation publishes a

Directory of Grant-making Trusts which costs £45 and is obtainable in most large reference libraries. It also publishes small paperback books for donors, listing organizations devoted to specific causes such as cancer relief, the blind, the deaf, animals and drug addicts, for example. If you feel you have a chance of obtaining a grant, it is worth sending for the very helpful leaflet which the Foundation publishes that tells you how to set about applying.

If you have any large companies or industrial concerns in your locality, these can prove very fertile ground for donations. Some firms are so switched on to play an active part in all the good work going on around them that they have a charities committee, sometimes chaired by one of the directors. Relief on corporation tax may be granted to companies making a charitable donation to a trade-related cause (the upkeep of a retirement home, for instance) or to any local charity: the fire service benevolent fund is one such example.

Another important way in which business firms may contribute to the work you are doing is by making gifts in kind, with the possible spin-off of publicity for their brand name or logo. Never miss a chance to invite firms to donate not only money but furniture, furnishings, appliances, equipment, tools, a vehicle, building materials, and so on. Whatever you need for your project, there is always someone somewhere who will be pleased to donate it or at the very least sell it to you at a favourable discount: a vanload of off-cuts of marine ply timber suitable for cladding stalls for the fête; bags of odds and ends of quilted material, just the job for dolls' clothes; ex-demonstration kitchen appliances – all these have come the way of various committees as a 'makeweight' following on a letter seeking a donation.

Just as the pile of pennies starts with a single coin and climbs to almost unbelievable heights, so small 'voluntary payment' schemes, organized in factories and stores, are of inestimable value to appeal funds. One such scheme started for the St Francis Hospice Development Trust at Havering-atte-Bower near Romford in Essex brings large-scale fund-raising right on to the factory floor. Workers at Ford's and other nearby industrial plants operate a weekly 'pay-as-you-earn' collection to help with the massive yearly running costs of the hospice; about £600,000 a year to support fifteen beds and, eventually, a home-care service. The money is deducted from employees' wages (it could of course be collected in cash) and sent each month to the appeal fund. This reassuringly regular income can help turn a dream into a reality.

To set up a scheme of this kind, write in the first place to the chairman or managing director of the firm and, if appropriate, invite him to see the development, the site, the plans or whatever. Then, with his blessing and permission (and, it is hoped, a donation as well), you can invite the secretary of the works social club, the union shop stewards or other representatives. Fund-raising is not only about raising money, it is about involving the whole community in a caring way, and this is a splendid way to do it.

The community, of course, includes the banks, and often the bank can prove to be the appeal organizer's best friend. Some banks even loan out employees close to retirement to take charge of charity accounts. One banker I know, with two years to go before he was due to draw his pension, was offered (by the bank) a list of five charity funds to manage. Being a quiet sort of chap who loved the country and a spot of weekend birdwatching, he chose a naturalist trust. He is as happy as a sandboy in this role, and looks more at home in sweater and cords than ever he did in a city suit.

Small children staggering into a bank under the weight of huge bags of coins and fund-raising organizers dropping by with suitcases full of cash to be counted are just part of the picture. Banks serve as a clearing point for appeals envelopes and handle charities' accounts without charging interest, as well as offering free advice.

If you are running a large event and expect to take several hundred pounds during the day, it is worth asking your bank if it would set up an office on site – backstage in the hall, or in a caravan on the field – for receiving and accounting for the money.

Until I began work on this book, and started asking questions, I had not realized that a large annual bazaar where I usually sell teddy-bears or tin whistles enjoys banking services all day on Saturday.

'It's just one of the ways we can made a contribution locally,' the manager told me with a matter-of-fact shrug, as if everybody surely knew that. I certainly didn't.

Whenever you are handling money for an appeal fund or an organization of any kind, from something on the scale of Live Aid to a local jumble sale, it is best to work on a proper financial footing, open an account at the bank and keep a set of simple accounts.

If you are accumulating money which is to be paid over in one amount – saving it up, in other words – a deposit account, which pays interest, is one of your options; you could, alternatively, invest it in a building society, unit trust or other scheme. If your organization will have to pay out cash, as well as receive it – in expenses for helpers who have bought ingredients, for example – you will need the facility of a cheque book.

Banks will advise you to nominate at least two people from the committee who must both sign the cheques; if there are three authorized signatories, two must sign; if there are four, three must, and so on. Of course you may have an account requiring a single signature – there is no law against it – but if you do so you run the risk of some grossly uncharitable person initiating an embarrassing dispute which can only harm your enterprise and divert people's energies from the cause itself.

To open an account you need declaration forms (provided by the bank) for the officers, members or helpers of the organization. These are completed both when an account is opened and whenever there needs to be a change of signatory: at the annual general meeting when new officers are appointed, for example, or when someone moves away.

In the case of the accounts you keep, there is one golden rule: keep them simple. Unless you have a bookkeeping expert in your midst, top-heavy administration can be confusing. Having said that, the accounts must be not only accurate but comprehensible – even to someone like me, sitting in the back row at the committee meeting and trying to grasp whether the amount of 'cash in hand' will pay in advance for the hire of the hall, or whether we will have to rustle up a coffee morning to pay our way.

On any committee there is always someone who wants

to be treasurer. It is part of his or her job to ask for receipts for every item of expenditure, however small. When I am buying ingredients for food items to be sold for charity I keep an envelope, pop every little check-out receipt into it, list every bridge roll and quarter of mushrooms, and hand it all over to the treasurer before the event; if I am selling tickets for a function, I list the numbers of tickets sold, plus the names, and whether any were at reduced price for children (it is odd how something as simple as that can completely throw the balance at the end). And I never let any tickets out of my possession until they are paid for (the people who were going to pay on the night are always the ones who get 'flu and cannot make it after all).

The limit of my own accounting ability is to make up my own list, expenditure on one side and receipts on the other, and hand it over. In the fullness of time, at the next committee meeting, Mr Moneybags solemnly presents for perusal an account of a single event, or the year's financial activity, and before the AGM has the accounts audited by a friendly neighbourhood banker.

Myself, I'd rather be the chap who pushes over the pile of pennies.

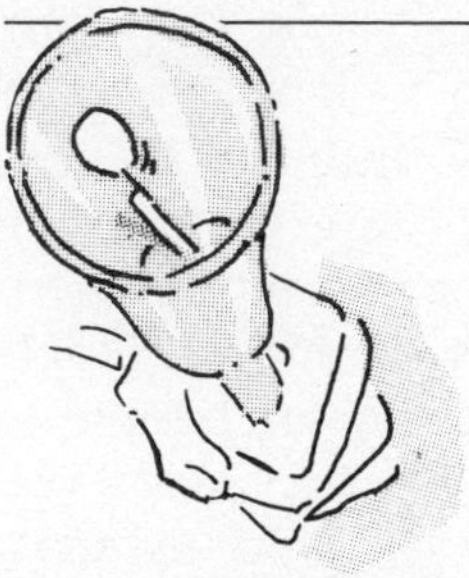

CHAPTER 11

Oyez! Oyez!

Think of publicity as a pebble. As soon as you have decided to hold an event of any kind, you drop the pebble into the pool. The ripples start to spread, and go on spreading. Just how far and wide they reach will have a direct bearing on how many people offer to help you, how many turn up to support the function, and how much money you make. So you'd better be sure to make it a big pebble, and drop it from a great height.

Publicity, like charity, begins at home. It is quite amazing – and quite unforgiveable – how many events take place without the people who should be most closely concerned knowing a thing about them – members of the club or association, or those who have shown their support and interest in the past. The saddest music in a fund-raiser's ears should be the phrase, 'If only I had known'.

So cover this eventuality first. That is the way to draw together the greatest numbers and get the team spirit working from the very outset. If the event is to raise funds for a school, club or hospital, make sure that all the interested parties are among the first to know about it. As soon as the date is fixed, put an advance information poster on the notice-board giving an outline of the function and asking for offers of help where they are needed – providing cakes, jumble, muscle-power or whatever. Ask the head teacher if children may take home a note about it, so that you can involve the parents from the beginning, not just those on the committee. If you are part of an organization that has a mailing list, time the next newsletter to members so that you can announce this most important news item. How many mail shots have gone out the week before the meeting at which a fund-raising event was fixed? If this should happen to you, you will either have to mail them all again, writing off the cost of postage to experience, or hope – forlornly – that people will hear of it through the grape-vine. If the event is also a social gathering for members and friends, mention it as a 'come on' in letters sent out to remind people about the annual subscriptions. It is good for people to know, as they write out their yearly cheques, that you want the pleasure of their company as well as their money! Put a small photocopied slip inside any brochure that is going out to 'Friends' of the organization. If there is to be a meeting of any part of the association or fringe group connected with it, give the chairman a notice of the event so that he or she can read it out under 'any other business'. People can then put the date in their diaries if they are interested, and keep it free. It makes the job of the ticket-sellers a lot easier when the time comes if people have had early warning.

This constitutes the first ripple, well and truly spread round a close circle of people who all share your interest and concern for the cause.

Maybe your committee already has a publicity officer. If not, perhaps you should appoint one. Situation vacant. Wanted: someone who is committed to the cause. Has a little time to spare and is prepared to squeeze in a little more when the occasion arises; someone who never takes no for an answer, who can think laterally, visualize glorious schemes and convey that enthusiasm to others who may not have the same powers of imagination; who ideally has a few established contacts in the local press or other media already, or who, if successful in the application for this job, soon will have; who can write imaginative, concise and readable copy that busy newspaper journalists can print without altering a word (that is important: that way, fewer mistakes will creep in!); who knows where to go to get posters, handbills, catalogues and tickets printed cheaply and quickly – and is prepared to put pressure on the printer to stick to the agreed deadline; and who pays meticulous attention to detail – dates, times, admission prices, charity to benefit, and so on. It is not unknown for notices advertising forthcoming events to be produced and distributed door to door before anyone realizes that the date and time have not been mentioned. A few specially interested people will telephone to make a hesitant enquiry. Most will not bother, and will stay away in large numbers.

Do not be surprised if you do not have a queue of applicants for the post, even though it is one of the most stimulating and exciting of all. Some publicity officers are born (you can spot them a mile off at a meeting – they are the ones who keep coming up with ideas, some a bit on the outrageous side, perhaps, but at least it shows they are trying). Some are appointed, and do an adequate job. Their functions make an adequate amount of money. If you cannot find anybody to take on the responsibility single-handed, and it is a big function you are planning, split up the tasks between several supporters, one to deal with the printing, one to contact the press and so on. It is not ideal, but it can work perfectly well, as long as they all keep in close touch.

Once your bandwagon gets rolling, some of the best publicity will come free. Even so, you will need a budget for printing tickets, posters, handbills and car stickers; to cover any special effects such as T-shirts and floats; and to pay for press advertising. The budget should clearly be in reasonable proportion to the hoped-for profit. There is a wise old saying that you have to speculate to accumulate. There should also be one to the effect that it is madness to speculate in a grand manner if a large-scale profit just is not there to be made. As in all business ventures – and putting on a function of any kind is very much that – you have to strike the right balance.

What if yours is a new undertaking and there is no money in the kitty to start with? You cannot take a publicity budget out of a zero bank balance. However, you *could* raise a loan from one of the members against the ticket sales, and then repay it from the funds once the money starts coming in. But I find this an untidy way to keep the books. It is far better to organize a small pre-function function to give you a starting balance: something that does not involve supporters in too much work – you want to conserve their energies for the big one – and will be likely to appeal to a fairly wide audience. This is not the time to stretch originality to the nerve-ends – a coffee morning, sherry morning, jumble sale or something with a tried and tested format fills the bill admirably. You will find information and advice on jumble sales and other small money-raisers starting on page 120; for coffee mornings and sherry parties see pages 110-11.

What's in a name? A tremendous amount. The way you choose to describe your fund-raising event is the first major step in your publicity drive. The name you choose should give the event personality, character, originality, memorability, ticket saleability and press appeal. Unlikely as it may seem, just this simple decision can have a devastating effect on the eventual success of the venture. The name immediately builds up an image in people's minds and helps to shape their opinion of the function. A run-of-the-mill name can, quite unfairly, make people think it will be a fairly pedestrian affair, whereas a bright and lively one gives them the impression that they will be in for a really good time, and missing something if they do not attend. Same event. Same venue. Same menu. But a name with a glint of humour or spark of atmosphere can be the make-or-break element, the key to success or failure.

This means that you have to decide how to christen the function practically before it is born. The name will be the first line people catch sight of as they drive past an advertising poster, the type that jumps out and catches their attention as someone hands them a ticket or handbill. Either they get a good first impression, and feel drawn towards the event, or they do not. It is as simple and as harsh as that.

Let us drop in on a committee meeting at which the members are planning to hold a supper party in the village hall. The poor old building is on its last legs, and is badly in need of a new roof. The hope is that it will stay wind- and waterproof long enough to give shelter to a thrash for 120 or so people this autumn. Someone volunteers to take charge of the catering and straight away details people to join a sub-committee. Everyone agrees that cold turkey and ham with a choice of salads and puddings will be ideal, with hot soup to start with, just in case there is a nip in the air by then. Someone else agrees to get the tickets printed. There is no publicity officer, or he would doubtless have come along with a list of ideas to put to the meeting. And off they all go, confident that as long as the catering ladies know how much coleslaw to make for the assembled company, everything is under control.

Well, it is not. You go round trying to sell those tickets a week or so later and see the blank looks you get. 'The Village Hall Committee are holding a Supper Party. In the Hall. Saturday 29 September. 8 o'clock. Ticket, £4.' By the time you have met with the tenth mumbled apology, or at best the promise to 'let you know in a few days', you begin to wonder whether by any unlucky chance you have hit on the evening of the Royal Command Performance – and the whole neighbourhood has been invited to attend in person. Or it could just be that you have not fired their imaginations in that subtle, almost indefinable way. By the name.

It is always uphill work trying to persuade people they should attend something just because it is in a good cause. And it should not be necessary. *You* know that your event is going to be the most tremendous fun. It is just a question of conveying that message in a couple of well-chosen words.

There are certain evocative words connected with food. Manufacturers who produce everything from flour and biscuits to frozen dinners and canned soups know these words only too well. Farmhouse. Country. Home-made. Harvest. Old-fashioned. Have you noticed how they crop up in brand names and TV advertisements over and over again? They are chosen by people who are investing their all in the success of a new product. Viewers could be forgiven for thinking that nearing the end of the twentieth century we all live our lives in a haze of morning dew and sepia. But there must be a moral somewhere.

There is. Let us look again at the forthcoming attraction. It is a supper party, to be held in the autumn, in the village hall. Play around with words; many people find it easiest to get to grips with the problem if they scribble out a list. Just keep putting down words and phrases, linking this word with that, that word with this until you hit on something that sounds right. Harvest Home. Harvest Thanksgiving. Farmhouse Fare. Farmhouse Supper. Harvest Supper. Countryman's Supper. You do not need to live in the depths of the country to create the atmosphere of wholesome goodness – and that is what sells, nowadays.

The name you eventually choose can generate ideas for the design of the posters, tickets and so on. Most printers have a small stock of line drawings that can easily and cheaply be incorporated into your design and will hammer home the name still further. Invite your supporters to a Harvest Home supper, dangle a couple of tickets decorated with a wheatsheaf under their noses and you are more than half-way to making a sale – and a good profit.

Approach it another way. If the committee decides to get the party off to a good start with a 'free' drink as soon as people arrive, make it sparkle. Offer a glass of orange juice and bubbly white wine and call it, enticingly, a Buck's Fizz party. And, for good measure, play the appropriate tapes too. Or go the whole hog, serve a glass of real (or pretend) bubbly and bill the occasion as a Champagne Supper. It is quite amazing how that simple ploy pays dividends time and again.

Go back to the reason for the party, the poor old roof. There is plenty of food for thought there. Steeplejacks' Supper. Restoration Supper – that will intrigue the historians among your group. Roof-Rack Party. Make a list of words around that theme and see what you come up with. I guarantee you will never be satisfied with a boring, plain old supper party again.

Coffee mornings and sherry parties, often looked on as the Cinderellas of fund-raising events, do have their own special slot in a money-making campaign. They are useful, as we have seen, for providing a quick up-front cash balance without taxing energy resources to the full. They are good getting-to-know-you occasions, too, when a committee or team of helpers can draw in other friends and neighbours to meet socially and informally, and raise a bit of money into the bargain. The trouble is that in any community there do tend to be rather a lot of them, for the church, the Brownies, the flower club, the political associations, the women's organizations, and so on.

Make your event the one that stands out head and shoulders above the crowd, and draws in the supporters and the funds. Just by what you call it. Invite people to 'Café Filtre and Croissants' or a Brazilian Coffee Bash. Tell them on the tickets that 'Coffee will be percolating all morning at 32 Dawn Avenue' and they will be able to smell those beans already.

Sherry parties are not high on my list of fun things to do – I find the golden nectar rather too heady, and often far too cloying. Water down the drinks a bit (and bump up the profits) with a Sherry-on-the-Rocks party, which is now more the 'in thing', and particularly acceptable on a warm day. It does not have to be sherry, though, does it? Order a couple of cases of rosé wine and hand out pink cards enticing friends to come to a Pink Plonk Party. They will be intrigued. And they'll come.

Children like to deal in superlatives, and the more superlative the better. Any function that is designed to attract the youngsters does well to have a massive 'handle'. Mammoth this or gigantic that. Supercolossal Toy Fair. Fantastic Fun Fair. Ginormous Jumble Sale. Star-trek Treasure Hunt. It is easier to sell lollipops to children if you stage an event that talks their language right from the start.

If the event is to be an 'everybody welcome' affair, like a bazaar, jumble sale, fête or toy fair, you want to shout it from the rooftops, and part of your publicity budget may go on posters. Lesson number 1 here is that posters are designed to be read, and must be easily readable at a reasonable distance. Several factors affect readability: the size of the poster, of course, the size and actual design of the type (what printers call the typeface), the colour of the paper or card, and the colour of the printing ink. Sunshine yellow and lime green on a white ground may create just the joys-of-spring feeling you are trying to get across; the only trouble is that no one will actually be able to read it. I would not go so far as to say that elections are won and lost by the poster campaign (oh, that it were as simple as that!), but poster-spotting at the time of an election is a very interesting pastime. If you happen to go on a longish drive, crossing from one constituency to another, you will see that some posters are a great deal more effective (in terms of presentation, not policy) than others. Another point to watch is that some poster inks fade more readily than others, and it is as well to take the advice of the printer. He will know which customers have complained in the past that their carefully thought out message was here for all to read one day, and faded almost into oblivion the next.

Poster design is an art in itself. If there is anyone in your group who has had art training, or has a good eye for this kind of thing, then you are home and dry. If not, it is a good idea to ask one of the art teachers at the local school or college if they could suggest someone who would take on the job on a freelance basis. If you find someone who is willing, do not make their job impossible by giving them a complete essay to get into a piece of card 20 x 15 inches. The golden rule is to limit the display to the basic facts: the description of the event, date, time, place, cause, admission fee and any special attractions, as far as possible all in words of one syllable.

An artist who is sympathetic to your particular good cause may be prepared to rush off a dozen or so posters by hand, either as a contribution or for a reasonable fee. For a larger order, or if you cannot locate a tame designer, take your poster and your problem to the local printers. They will almost certainly have a drawer full of previous designs they have carried out, and you can choose the size and colour combinations you want from examples in front of you.

Much the same goes for handbills and leaflets. Again, keep the message visually clear and simple. People tend to be put off by a lengthy and cramped text and your words of wisdom may well meet their end in the wastebin.

Good poster sites are like gold dust in any community, and everyone connected with your organization will know where they are. House windows, shop windows and trees in someone's garden or on farmland are naturals, and may be yours for a polite word of asking. Lamp-posts and telegraph poles are not fair game – that counts as fly-posting. Ask the clerk to the parish council or town council for permission to pin up a poster on council property such as the parish notice-board. If it advertises a charity function there should be no problem: if the function is in aid of a political party, permission is not likely to be forthcoming. Try to get a good 'spread' of sites: windows, gates and doors people pass on their way to the post office or local supermarket, ones near bus-stops, school gates, the hall where the play-group is held, or close to the entrance of the car park. Trees or gates on the approach roads to the locality need to be well covered, too, and remember to have posters facing motorists travelling in both directions.

Cast about for any unusual sites, and at the same time consider the question of vulnerability. Posters often fall victim to mischief, if not vandalism. Have some spares in reserve to replace any that are damaged or stolen, so that your campaign can continue without interruption. For posters sited in open ground you will need stout stakes supporting a piece of hardboard or bonded board. Get a handyman on the committee to make them. Often local woodyards or DIY suppliers will give you off-cuts without charging. Then, after the event, store them for next time round.

If I were asked to give a prize for the best-ever poster site it would go to one I passed daily on my way to the station. I can see it now, the poster firmly atop a massive post in splendid and easy-to-read isolation, bang in the middle of a private pond close to the road. I noticed, however, that it stayed there for a very long time after the event.

A last word on the subject of posters: do cover outdoor ones against the elements by sticking or nailing polythene sheeting over them or enclosing poster boards in large plastic bags (the kind you get from the dry cleaner's are useful). Then, come hail or high water, your message will still get across.

If you decide to have advertising handbills, which people can take home, read at their leisure and refer to once they have forgotten the date, there are various ways of distributing them. There are the local roundsmen, who will often oblige when it is for a good cause by putting one in every door with the delivery. Or you can have teams of youngsters putting them on the windscreens of parked cars or handing them out in the market or shopping precinct on Saturdays.

Here is a chance to have some fun and create more of an impact. Ask teenagers or members of the club to dress up to draw attention to the event. They could wear vaguely Victorian dress to hand out notices about an old-time eye-catching outfit of the St Trinian's girls to drum up enthusiasm for a PTA event, the most fetching of sports gear when there is going to be a fun run, and so on.

Carry the idea further – as far as imagination and inventiveness will go. Your chorus of happy publicists can be pushing a decorated pram around the precinct; pedalling along on a tricycle; jogging in track-suits; handing out printed balloons (Toy Town Fair, 15 December); trailing streamers, 'just-married' style, from a cavalcade of cars; or, if energy and enthusiasm run to it, chugging through the town on a tractor and trailer, a traditional carnival float, handing out leaflets like confetti. Do not forget that whenever unusual use of the road is involved, so are the police. Notify them well in advance.

When there are high profits at stake and you have a nucleus of natural supporters, such as members of a sports club, it might be worth considering having a message emblazoned on T-shirts. It is a relatively cheap but quite powerful form of advertising. In similar vein, think of having badges printed with a long-term message, such as 'Adopt a Window' for the church restoration fund appeal, or 'The Lions Need a Home' for the football pavilion. Also effective are car stickers advertising a bazaar or fête.

Never overlook the power of the press. If your budget can run to it, take an advertisement in the 'What's on' pages of the local paper to let everyone know about your forthcoming event. Lots of people scour the papers to see where they can hope to pick up a bargain, have a day out with the children, shelter from the weekend thunderstorms, or enjoy the summer weather. Many newspaper proprietors have a policy of offering half-price advertisements for charities and accredited good causes (even the scouts' jumble sale comes into that category), but if you have to pay the full price it is usually money well spent.

If you consider your event worth spending money on, in the form of a newspaper advertisement, the chances are that the editorial staff will consider it worth a few column inches, though there is no guarantee. This is where the publicity officer comes in. At least two or three weeks before the event, send in a news item that conveys the atmosphere of the event and sets the scene. If you have a theme, as for a Hallowe'en bazaar, warn that people shopping in the market should be on the look-out for giant black cats and witches on broomsticks casting spells on potential customers. If it is a Red Riding Hood toy fair, capture the readers' imagination by telling them that this time you are really going to paint the town hall red – they will wake up one Saturday morning and find that it has disappeared under a cloud of red balloons, jazzy lighting and scarlet streamers, and appears to be completely in the hands of nursery-book characters provided by the local dancing school.

If you are having a personality to open the event, judge a competition, give prizes or take part in some other way, you have a Heaven-sent opportunity for publicity. That is of course why you decided to invite him (or her). Keep your eyes and ears open well in advance of the function. Perhaps your star-for-a-day is opening in a new series on television or a stage play, has just come back from a fact-finding tour in Africa, or has had a new book published. Draw the attention of your local news editor to this. A news item that Cheryl Cherry, who will be opening the fête on Saturday week in the rectory garden, has done such-and-such marvellous thing will notch up another useful mention of your event.

Ask the personality's agent, manager or secretary, again in plenty of time, for two or three black-and-white photographs that you can use for publicity purposes. If he or she is a local MP, councillor or personality, the newspapers will have some on file. Otherwise, send in a print to each newspaper when you send a story. Every picture tells even more of a story, so it will very probably be used.

Check, and check again before the event, whether the guest speaker is prepared to give interviews to newspaper, radio and TV reporters during or after the proceedings. If the answer is yes, as it should be, write this into any letter of agreement or contract you send. If it is no, say thank you politely and turn to the next guest on your list. I was once badly let down in this way by a television personality-turned-politician who was one of the principal protagonists at the Dunmow Flitch Trials. It had been agreed in black and white that he would talk to the press, yet when I approached him after the main event with three or four national press interviewers, notebooks and tape recorders at the ready, he refused.

'Anything like that will have to be the subject of a separate contract' (more money, he meant) 'negotiated three weeks in advance with my agent.' And off he stalked.

A publicity officer's lot is *usually*, but not always, a happy one.

Whenever a major speech is to be made, whether by an outside guest, the president or chairman of your organization or someone else, ask if it would be possible to have a copy of it, or an extract of a few sentences, so that it can be ready to incorporate into the news report. It saves misunderstandings, mistakes and some individual's discomfort while trying to take shorthand notes under an umbrella in the middle of a field in a howling gale.

If there is a local flying club in the vicinity, approach the secretary and ask whether any of its members could be persuaded to fly suitably low trailing a banner advertising your venture. Heads always turn skywards when there is the throb, throb, throb of an aircraft engine on the horizon. People might as well catch a fleeting glimpse of the date, time and place of your Barbecue Bonanza before they turn back to watering the garden.

If you do not do so already, start listening in to your local radio station – always a marvellous means of two-way communication. Note the kind of announcements made and find out where yours could slot in. Perhaps they have a regular 15 minutes of local about-town news in the morning, a going-places spot with a regular presenter, or a weekly diary of events. If the radio station is within reasonable reach, call in there and write out your message. Most of them have printed forms at the reception desk, so that you can fill in the details clearly and concisely. Otherwise, write out the relevant factors so that you do not forget any important detail and phone your announcement through to the reception desk. You can be sure of a cheery word of welcome – friendly people, radio personnel – and a wide audience for your message.

If your event verges on the bizarre – witness the pink fairies and black widow spider escapades in the chapter on sponsorship – the publicity world is your oyster. Yes, let your local newspapers and radio and TV stations in on the secret. A chirpy radio or TV presenter might like to interview his first-ever spider-in-distress or arrange to bump into a hapless pink fairy as part of an outside broadcast. It is an outside chance, but one worth taking. It always pays to remember that people with sheets and sheets of newspaper and hours and hours of air time to fill need interesting stories, just as much as fund-raising events need and deserve publicity.

Once you have captured the hearts and minds of the local press in advance of the event, they will probably send a reporter and photographer to cover it. If by any chance they do not, and you do not have a publicity officer, detail a couple of your supporters to become journalist and cameraman for the day. Ask someone to be responsible for writing an accurate and detailed report. This means taking down the names, ages (if it is a children's event) and addresses of any prize-winners, and being on the spot when photographs are taken so that accurate captions can be provided. It also means making sure the report mentions the charity or good cause, the sum needed and the amount raised, and includes a couple of pertinent quotes from any guest speaker. 'Summer fête raises £200 towards £2000 pool for handicapped children' conveys to readers that this was a jolly good effort, but more money is urgently needed. You never know, it might bring in an unsolicited donation or two.

Time is of the essence with newspaper reports and photographs and you must find out beforehand when the deadline is. For an event held over the weekend you have not a moment to lose. Many newspapers want the material in on Monday or by Tuesday morning at the latest for the weekend edition, which has usually been distributed by the Thursday. This means getting a print done by an amateur photographer on Sunday, or rushing the film into an express processing service on the Monday. It also means typing up the report, on plain paper and in double spacing, while you are still recovering from all the exertions of the day. Tough!

Be sure to add a contact name and address so that someone on the staff can get in touch for further details.

(Who knows, with an event as successful as yours will be, it might make a front-page story.)

Some people regard writing press reports as something of a mystery, only to be undertaken by cub journalists wearing beige macs and flat caps. For the record, here are a couple of examples, one to announce a forthcoming attraction, and one to report on a recent success.

CHERYL LAUNCHES FORTH

The TV comedy actress Cheryl Cherry, best-known for her starring role in *Over the Rainbow*, is getting into practice at the Stadium Theatre this week. She is opening in a new play, *I Name This Ship*, on Thursday, and will soon be known as the lady who launches nine ships a week in Wigborough.

All this will stand her in good stead for opening the Boys' Brigade Bonanza at 2 pm in the playing field on Saturday.

Besides the produce and cake stalls, fairground side-shows and children's fancy-dress competition, there will be a display of dog-handling by a team from Chelsborough Police Station, and a good-natured game of cops and robbers. Admission is 35p; children 15p.

ROBINS ARE GETTING AROUND

You can hardly hear yourself think nowadays in Rotten End for the scratching of pens and the clicking of needles. The local children, whose ages range from seven to 13, have formed the Robin Club, an arts and crafts association, to raise money for Guide Dogs for the Blind.

The children held an inaugural meeting, formed a committee and set to work. In less than five weeks they held their first sale of work on Saturday, at Spices.

While home-made cakes, sweets and toys sold like hot cakes, pride of place was given to the book-stall-with-a-difference. The difference? They had written all the books themselves, so each one was a signed first edition.

> Their efforts raised £85 towards a guide dog which has been adopted by local residents. Fired with enthusiasm, the children have already planned their next venture, an art exhibition to be held in the village hall on 17 November. Coke and cakes will be available, and all exhibits will be for sale.

Oyez! Oyez! All ye who are gathered here, do not forget that publicity has a long and noble heritage. Long before newspapers rolled off the presses or transistor radio sets kept us in touch with what is going on, the town crier went round in his eye-catching uniform, ringing his ear-catching bell, and making announcements at the top of his voice.

The town crier in the Suffolk-border village where I lived was a cunning old monkey who certainly knew a thing or two about publicity. The lady up at the big house would send a note round saying she had lost her gold bracelet between X Manor and Y Hall on Tuesday afternoon and there would be a handsome reward for anyone who found it. Our man, complete with red frock coat and black velour hat, would rush down there, scrabble about in the undergrowth and pocket the precious article. Then he would cry the tidings round the village. Bad news! Bad news! After a suitable interlude, he would return the bracelet and collect both his town crier's fee *and* the reward.

If you are lucky enough to have a town crier anywhere near you, do rope him in to cry the glad tidings of your coming event in the market-place, shopping precinct or from the steps of the town hall, or engage him on the day. He will certainly attract attention.

Useful addresses

Registering a charity
To apply to register as a charity an organization formed to raise money for a good cause, write giving full details to The Registration Section, Charity Commission, 14 Ryder Street, London SW1.

Music licences
To apply for a licence to play music recorded by any means, and in premises which are not already licensed, write giving full details to Phonographic Performance Ltd, Ganton House, 14 Ganton Street, London W1. The payment of a fee is usually waived in the case of registered charities.

To apply for a licence to play live music in premises which are not already licensed, write giving full details to The Performing Right Society, 29 Berners Street, London W1. The payment of a fee is usually waived in the case of registered charities.

Aid from trust funds
To apply for donations to a registered charity from a trust fund (see page 140), write giving full details to Charities Aid Foundation, Crane Court, Fleet Street, London EC4.

Hiring props
For anything from Father Christmas suits to tombola drums, coconut shies, roll-a-ball-games, Hallowe'en skeletons (full-size) and balloon pumps (all of which can be hired), or to buy garlands, streamers, party poppers (streamers that shoot out with a bang), balloons printed with your own message, hats, crackers, flags, bunting, rosettes, masks (you think of it, they have it), write for a catalogue to Barnum's Carnival Novelties Ltd, 67 Hammersmith Road, London W14 8UY.